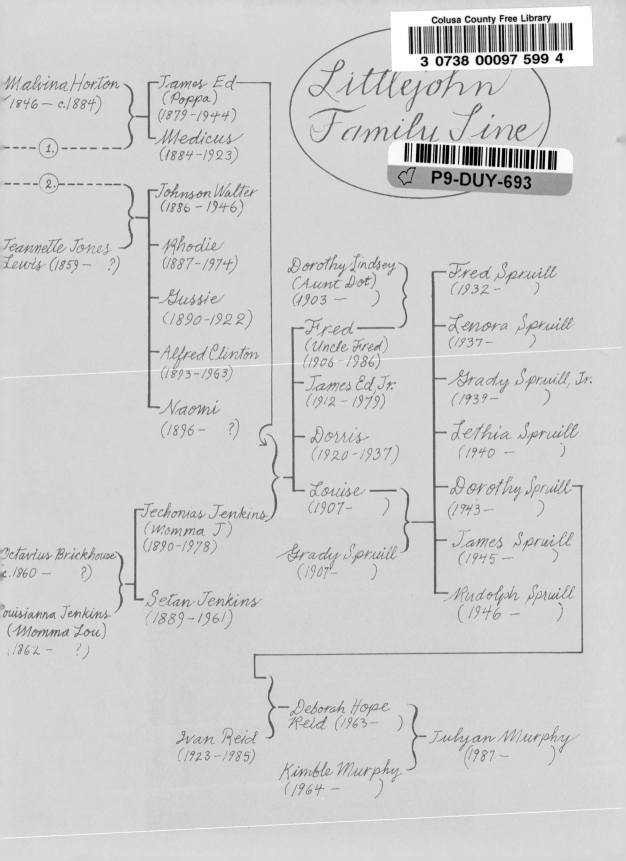

SOMERSET
HOMECOMING

DOROTHY SPRUILL REDFORD
WITH MICHAEL D'ORSO

SOMERSET HOMECOMING
RECOVERING A LOST HERITAGE

INTRODUCTION BY ALEX HALEY

Doubleday

NEW YORK   LONDON   TORONTO   SYDNEY   AUCKLAND

Grateful acknowledgment is made to Senator Clarence W. Blount for permission to quote from his November 1986 letter to Dorothy Spruill Redford.

Published by Doubleday, a division of
Bantam Doubleday Dell Publishing Group, Inc.,
666 Fifth Avenue, New York, New York 10103

Doubleday and the portrayal of an anchor with a dolphin
are trademarks of Doubleday, a division of
Bantam Doubleday Dell Publishing Group, Inc.

Library of Congress Cataloging-in-Publication Data
Redford, Dorothy Spruill.
Somerset homecoming.

1. Somerset Place (N.C.)—History.   2. Afro-
Americans—North Carolina—History.   3. Slavery—North
Carolina—History.   4. Family reunions—North Carolina.
5. Afro-American families.   6. Afro-Americans—
Genealogy.   7. North Carolina—Genealogy.   I. D'Orso,
Michael.   II. Title.
E185.96.R42   1988   929'.3'089960730756   87-35155

ISBN 0-385-24245-X

ACKNOWLEDGMENTS

A traditional saying among my people is "Praise the bridge that carries you over." During the past eleven years, ever since Alex Haley's *Roots* inspired my search that culminated in the 1986 Somerset Homecoming, I have crossed many waters—some deep, some stagnant, some muddy—but strong, supportive bridges were always there for me. Among them:

· All of the scholars whose published works provided information, insight and instruction . . . and some who lent an ear and encouragement: James Proctor Brown (Norfolk State University), Eric Ayisi (College of William and Mary) and Peter Wood (Duke University).

· The offices of the Clerk of Courts for Chowan, Tyrrell and Washington counties in North Carolina.

- The Sargent Memorial Room of the Kirn Library, Norfolk, Virginia.
- The North Carolina State Archives and the staff of the Search Room, who assisted me in accessing the Josiah Collins family papers.
- The Northeastern North Carolina Historic Places Office, which provided a grant to photocopy more than two thousand pages from the Collins Collection and house them at Somerset Place.
- My friends in the Historic Sites Section of the North Carolina Department of Cultural Resources, who worked tirelessly to ready the site and support the event.
- The many journalists whose coverage of the Homecoming allowed the nation to share in the healing effects of the day. And one journalist in particular, Mike D'Orso, features writer for the *Virginian-Pilot* and the *Ledger-Star,* through whose talents this volume was written. The staff of the *Virginian-Pilot* and the *Ledger-Star,* and especially the staff of the newspapers' library, for their support of his efforts in writing this book.
- My co-workers at the Portsmouth Department of Social Services and those other friends who on a daily basis applauded every small accomplishment and said, "We are proud of you."
- The strongest and most supportive bridges are family: my mother, father, brothers and sisters, and especially my daughter Deborah, for whom my love is unconditional, as is her love

and support for me. And then there is our extended family of Somerset Place descendants, who made the Homecoming a true celebration of life and a reaffirmation of family.

—*Dorothy Spruill Redford*

CONTENTS

INTRODUCTION

I had just gotten off a cargo ship in Antwerp, Belgium, after four weeks of writing at sea, and I was on a flight to Los Angeles when I saw a story in *USA Today* about Dorothy Redford and her reunion of slave descendants at a North Carolina plantation.

Dorothy had written to me several times over the previous years about her personal search for her own slave ancestors and her subsequent study of the plantation and its slave community. I had responded with encouragement and what advice I thought might help. When her last letter invited me to attend a homecoming at the site, I wrote back that I could not attend because of my own plans to be at sea.

Now, airborne back to America, I realized I had not yet missed the event. From her letters, I knew what a beautiful piece of work Dorothy had been developing, and I was excited at the possibility of our meeting, of seeing the site she had studied for so long and of witnessing the heartfelt, human gathering she had brought about.

When I got to Los Angeles, I showed the newspaper article to two lifelong friends of mine from our tiny hometown of Henning, Tennessee, and purely upon impulse, we caught the first plane to Norfolk. There we rented a car and drove south into the North Carolina countryside and finally arrived at the Somerset Place plantation in the midst of the celebration.

I was thrilled—thrilled not just at what was happening there that day, but for the connections that such a gathering of families spoke of—for the thread that ran back through the generations and will most surely run ahead into the future. To see those scores of families, all returned to the soil of their ancestors, resurrecting the spirit of their kin who came before, made me think of what, I believe, was certainly my most dramatic moment in the making of *Roots.*

We were in Savannah, Georgia, getting ready to film a scene where Kunta Kinte refused to call himself by the name his master had given him. The master had decided Kunta's name would be "Toby." The overseer was given the word, and he passed it to the old slave who was training the young Kunta.

The old slave was being played by Lou Gossett, and the young slave, of course, by Levar Burton. But no matter what the old slave did, the young one refused to accept another name. Finally, word of his defiance went back via the overseer to the master, who ordered Kunta beaten until he would say his new name was now "Toby."

That was the scene to be filmed that day. Levar was brought out and tied with his wrists to a set of crossed poles, much like an Indian tepee. As he hung there, to his right sat the old slave, Lou Gossett, who was being punished for his inability to get the young slave to say the name and who would be needed to help remove the young slave after what would surely be a terrible beating.

When the director announced "Action!" the overseer came out, dressed in a kind of cloak, proud and furious. He looked at the young one hanging up there by his wrists and he said, "What's your name, boy?"

Levar answered quietly, "Kunta."

Smirking, the overseer looked over at a tall, anonymous slave in the background who was holding a whip, and this slave walked out into camera range, raised his arm and began.

The whip they were using was made with loosely woven hemp, nothing that would hurt anybody. But a trained actor knows how to jerk the instant it touches his skin, making the force and sting of the blow appear painfully real. Levar took two blows, then a third, which, with the special effects people's blood capsules breaking, was almost too much to look at.

Then, again, the overseer asked, "What's your name, boy?" Again, now weakly, Levar said, "Kunta."

After three more blows, and more blood, the thirty-five or so of us just out of camera range were so angry we were ready to charge out there and choke somebody.

This time Levar, his head nodding to one side, with no strength left even to lift his chin, said, in a whisper, "Toby, master." And the overseer whirled about, proud, arrogant. *"Louder!* Let me hear it again. *What's your name, boy?"*

Barely, Levar whispered, "Toby, master."

Then the tall slave who had done the beating cut Levar down, and Levar slumped into Lou Gossett's lap.

Gossett, an experienced veteran actor, was supposed to embrace the young slave, to comfort him. One camera was to slowly slide out of focus, as an optional way to end that two-hour episode.

But what happened is something that people who spend their lives around films being made may witness but a few times—when experienced actors or actresses totally forget who they are and become the role they are portraying, letting what's inside them take over.

When Levar slumped into Lou Gossett's lap, Lou's own body began convulsing. He curled into a near-fetal position, grasping Levar to his own shaking self—and out of Lou's voice box, through his tears, came a hoarse, guttural cry.

"What *difference* it make what they calls you? You *knows* who you is, you's *Kunta!"*

He convulsed again. He let out another, even higher-pitched cry: "Dey's gonna be a better day."

He paused. Silence. Then he repeated it.

"Dey's gonna be a better day!"

Maybe ten seconds passed, then the last film was clicked through three cameras. The only sound was Lou's weeping.

Then he pulled himself back, out of the role, into the present. "I don't know what happened to me," he said. "I forgot about who I am. I was there, a hundred and fifty years ago, and that was my little Guinea boy. I was supposed to teach him how to be a slave and instead he had taught me how to be a man."

Years have gone by since that afternoon in Savannah, Georgia, but I have never been far from that cry or from those words: "They's gonna be a better day." Because that is the cry that was being cried by all the people—the black people, the white people, the red people, the other people living in the time that scene depicted. That was the cry that was heard on Somerset Place plantation, from one end to the other, and on every other plantation like it. That was the cry that came from people praying not just for themselves, but for their children and for all those who would follow them. That life would be better. That there would be a better day.

What compelled me to come to Somerset Place for its homecoming was to see that better day come alive in a setting like that. And it gave me the chance to witness what a marvelous thing my colleague has done. Dorothy's study is the best, most beautifully researched and most thoroughly presented black family history that I know of.

I don't believe I could imagine a better answer to the prayers of her relatives' foreparents—of *all* our foreparents—than what she has brought together and created at Somerset Place and the story she tells in these pages.

It is all our stories.

—*Alex Haley*

SOMERSET
HOMECOMING

Still yourself, hear your inner voice
and vigorously pursue its dictates.
When your purpose is noble—
when your goals benefit mankind—
all that you need to achieve them
will be available to you.

BEGINNINGS

Daddy was at work the windy February morning I came to ask about Columbia.

He was seventy then and holding down three jobs. The granary was closed. Waldo had shut it down back in 1962, after he became the city's Commissioner of Revenue. But Waldo didn't leave Daddy jobless. He took him along, made him a janitor, and that's where my father worked for the next thirteen years— keeping the Commissioner of Revenue offices clean.

They retired Daddy at sixty-five, but he wasn't the retiring kind. He'd been doing a man's work since he was twelve, and he wasn't about to sit down until he had to. So he got on as a runner at a local bank, was hired to clean a judge's office and clerked at a neighborhood hardware store. That was enough to keep his days filled.

Mother and he were living in town then, in Churchland proper, in a three-bedroom wood house Daddy built on land he paid for with some of his hogs. Six of us children were grown and gone. Rudolph, the youngest, was the only one still living at home. He was out, too, the morning I arrived to ask my mother who I was.

It was January 1977, a time when I had not been thinking much about the past.

I was thirty-three that winter, a single mother with a thirteen-year-old daughter. We lived in the South. Not the South of moss-draped oaks and whitewashed pillars—the snapshot images that spring to the mind of those who have not lived there. No, Deborah and I were in Portsmouth, Virginia, a gray harbor-front town of ships and sailors. I was a social worker, supervising three welfare offices that handled about a hundred cases a day. That was a good number, high enough to keep us all busy, knowing our jobs were secure. Sometimes it bothered me seeing my work that way, knowing my good fortune depended on someone else's bad. But I worked hard, and I was good at my job, good enough to think about moving that winter from our rented apartment to a townhouse—the first home Deborah and I could call our own.

My job, my daughter and a mortgage—I had plenty to think about but not so much not to know that the world was sitting down that week to watch "Roots." At least the world I knew. It was all my friends and co-workers could talk about. They

Louise and Grady Spruill, Dorothy Spruill Redford's parents. They were married in 1934.

watched it at night and talked about it in the morning—about Africa, about slavery, about finding their ancestors.

I was too busy with the here and now to think about there and then. But I watched, too. And as I did, it all rushed back, feelings I hadn't faced in years. Emptiness, anger, confusion, denial—most of all, denial. For thirteen years I had tucked those feelings away, telling myself they no longer mattered. Now they were back again, but with a difference. It wasn't just me facing the questions now. Deborah wanted answers, too. She watched, and suddenly she was asking about things we'd never talked about. Who were my great-grandparents? Where did they come from? Were they slaves? And *their* parents, where did *they* come from?

My daughter was demanding her past, but I could not give it to her without discovering my own. And that meant picking up where I left off the day Deborah was born. It meant going back to New York City, to Queens and Harlem, to Aunt Dot and Ivan.

Back to Virginia, to my mother and father and sisters and brothers, to hogs in the pen and prayers in the living room. Back to North Carolina, to a hazy town of dirt streets and distant cousins, to the edge of the woods where the vaguest family memories and whispered stories stopped—and beyond which my own story began.

That town in the woods was Columbia, North Carolina, where I was born in August 1943. My parents were not much for history, for talking about the old days. But they did reminisce now and then. And this much I knew:

It was a busy place, hard on the Scuppernong River, at the seacoast edge of the state. The black part of town had seven little streets—none of them paved—and the white part had ten. The Norfolk Southern tracks ran through the center of town, keeping white and black homes apart and stopping at the edge of the woods, where the sawmill sat. For the railroad, that mill was the end of the line, the place where the tracks ran out. But Columbia would not have been there without it. Lumber made that town. For generations, loggers from miles around drove or floated their timber to Columbia's mill, where it was cut and loaded onto boats headed seaward or railroad cars headed inland.

My mother always referred to Columbia as a "boom town." She'd talk about the out-of-town bus coming through, and the trains rolling in, the movie house, the store, the hotel where her great-uncle worked. None of the small surrounding villages had those things, so Columbia was the hub, the big time.

6

By the time I was born, most of the men in town—at least the black men—were gone. Some had left to war. Some had left for work somewhere else. And some had just left.

There were a few black professionals around: teachers, ministers, shop owners, and of course one of the most successful men in town—the undertaker. But if a job took more than muscle, it was most likely taken by a white. Blacks worked in the fields, digging potatoes for twenty cents an hour. Some women became domestics, cooking and cleaning for white families. The black men who were lucky handled freight for the railroad or got on at the log mill. And some of them found more than one way to make money off those logs. My grandmother would tell us about her husband searching the river for logs that had sunk, logs that really belonged to the sawmill. He'd fish them out, plane them and sell them on his own. There were men who earned their entire living just dredging up lost logs. There was no welfare in those days, so you did what you had to to get by.

My father went into the log woods—the thick pine forests where timber was cut—at twelve. A lot of boys just like him did the same thing, to support their mothers and sisters when the men were gone. My father's parents separated early on, so he and his mother took care of themselves and his sister. When he was old enough, my father got a job at the mill. By August 7, 1943, he was earning twelve dollars a week for fifty-six hours of work. That was the day I was born, and that was the day he left town.

It was a Saturday morning, and he and a white man named Leslie Snell decided to catch the bus to Virginia. There were already four children in our house, and my father could not support five on the pay he was getting. He had heard about a lumber mill up in Portsmouth that had big contracts with the Navy shipyard and plenty of jobs. So he just went. He left at eight in the morning, and I was born at two that afternoon, the only one of my mother's children to be delivered in a hospital. Old Doc Chapman, who delivered all the black and white babies in Columbia, always came to your house, gave you ether or whatever, and you bore your child right there. But not this time. I guess it was my mother's way of protest, being angry at my father leaving her behind, but she said, "Oh no, this one is going into the hospital." That's another thing that made Columbia a big town. It had the hospital. Seven beds.

So my father stayed in Portsmouth, earning forty-two dollars a week, sending money to my mother and coming home when he could—a four-hour bus ride in those days. We lived upstairs in the home of my mother's parents, Momma J and Poppa. Poppa wasn't working anymore. He was preaching. And Momma J, she was doing just whatever she'd ever done, which is not much of anything. She was in her own world, my mother would say.

I think Mother would have stayed in Columbia forever if Poppa hadn't died. But he got typhoid in 1944. My mother told me they put him in a front room of the house, with a cheesecloth net over his bed to keep the flies away from him. She said she

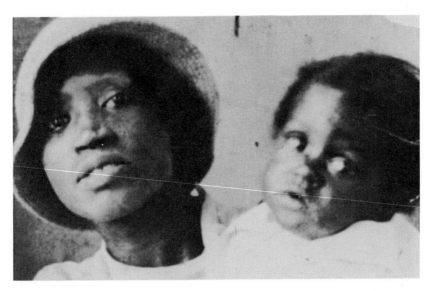

Louise Littlejohn Spruill, Dorothy's mother, in 1933, holding her oldest son, Fred.

could hear him breathing, hear his death rattle, hear him dying in that room.

When my mother packed us up and moved to join Daddy in 1945, she was pregnant with her sixth baby. And she was petrified. Back in Columbia, you walked everywhere. Nothing was more than a mile away. But here were things she had never seen before. She had never seen city buses. Stoplights. Traffic. She had been used to living in a large country house, with a big porch on the front and another on the back. A yard. Lots of room. And now she was in a two-bedroom rowhouse, squeezed up against houses full of strangers, sharing one bedroom with my father while the five of us slept in the other. There wasn't a lot of money, but more than that, we were living on pavement. There was no garden in the backyard. No field to go to for food.

No way to make do for yourself except to make money.

Daddy couldn't earn enough. And with another child on the way, his family needed room. My mother's brother, Uncle Fred, lived in New York City with his wife Dorothy, my namesake. She was "Big Dot," I was "Little Dot." They had no children, they had money and they had time. When they offered to keep me for a while, my parents sent me north for a summer that lasted eight years.

My own memories begin in New York. I remember sitting in an apartment in Queens, looking out on elevated railroad tracks. Later, we moved to a house with a yard. I remember Aunt Dot and Uncle Fred playing cards in the front room once a week, while I sat on the floor in front of a large radio, listening to "The Lone Ranger." I remember going to a concert and seeing men in sparkling red tuxedo jackets; I found out years later that one of those men was Count Basie. I remember Aunt Dot walking me to kindergarten every morning, and taking me to a movie every Wednesday afternoon.

Uncle Fred was my mother's oldest brother, a dark, tall man. And Aunt Dot was Momma J all over again. She was a small woman, light-skinned, just like Momma J. She had black curly hair that fell down to her waist, just like Momma J's. It was as if Uncle Fred had married his mother.

But there was more. Aunt Dot lived in a world far beyond Momma J's dreams. When you looked at Aunt Dot, you knew you were looking at a lady. She wore the finest clothes: a Persian lamb coat, a full-length mink. These were working people—

Uncle Fred had a job in a Manhattan cleaners—but Aunt Dot could squeeze a penny. Everything she bought had to be the very best, the most expensive she could find. And somehow she found a way to get it. In Aunt Dot's house, everything had to be just so. Even what we ate. Only the proper food—a salad every day. No fried foods, none of that Southern home cooking. On a special occasion we might have ham, but more often it was beef. At that time, if you ate beef that meant you were really living well. Real status. So we had hamburgers every Saturday, just like our Jewish neighbors. Fish every Friday, just like the Catholics. Mixed vegetables two nights a week. I still remember spitting those mixed vegetables back onto my plate. I hated mixed vegetables.

Aunt Dot and Uncle Fred were both from Columbia, but there was nothing on their dinner table that you'd see back in North Carolina. Nothing in their speech either, no Southern accent. They'd left all that behind when they came north in the late twenties. It had taken some time, but over the years they had managed to leave every bridge behind them in ashes. Back in Columbia, you were either black or white. And black meant black. There was no pecking order, no difference between fair skin and dark. Everyone was related. Everyone was linked. You can't discriminate on seven streets. But Aunt Dot and Uncle Fred came from two of the wealthier black families in town. They were used to feeling special. When they got to New York, however, they were nobody.

The worst thing you could be in New York, white or black, was

a Southerner. Southerners were slow, ignorant, shuffling country folk. And if you were a black Southerner, you were the lowest
of the low. Even the other blacks—the native New Yorkers, the
West Indians—sneered at the South. So Aunt Dot and Uncle
Fred did what they had to. Suddenly they were no longer from
North Carolina. Suddenly they were Dorothy and Fred Littlejohn from Jamaica.

Suddenly, they were "islanders."

There wasn't much to it, really. They were chameleons, taking
on the shades of their surroundings. And their surroundings
were mostly white. The Queens neighborhood where Uncle
Fred and Aunt Dot lived was almost suburban, closer to something in Virginia than in Manhattan. Stand-alone houses and
separate yards. And lots of whites. There were only three black
families on Aunt Dot and Uncle Fred's block. I used to play with
the daughter of the Jewish doctor who lived across the street.
Next door to us was my best friend Maryann, a little Italian girl.
These were the kids I played with, white kids. The school I went
to had more whites than blacks. We were the minority, but we
were accepted. We did what the "well-to-do" did. We took in
that matinee every Wednesday. We shopped at Gertz, the best
department store in Queens. I took dance lessons, wore hand-
knit sweaters, walked to school with a clean handkerchief pinned
to my left shoulder, was even left with a sitter when Aunt Dot
and Uncle Fred took a proper vacation. We were a model family,
right out of the books Aunt Dot liked to read. To our white

12

neighbors, to the white people Uncle Fred worked for, we were "okay" blacks. And Aunt Dot made sure we stayed that way.

But it wasn't easy. Not with me around. From the time I learned to speak, Aunt Dot spent each day praying I'd keep my mouth shut. Once a week we'd ride the subway into Manhattan, meet Uncle Fred after work and go out to dinner. Well-bred families did that. We'd meet Uncle Fred at the cleaners, and if there was one place the act counted, it was there, where Uncle Fred worked. Two days before we'd ride in, Aunt Dot would start the harping: *"Don't* tell them where you're from. *Don't* talk about Virginia." I knew where I was from. I knew I wasn't from any island. I knew Aunt Dot and Uncle Fred weren't either. And I was just the kind of little girl who would answer back: "Why can't I say what I want?" All the years I was there Aunt Dot lived in mortal terror, convinced I was going to pull the masks off.

When they had first come north, Uncle Fred had worked in a meat packing house. But before long he was hired as a spotter at a cleaners. And he wasn't just any spotter. He was a mid-Manhattan spotter, something special. He only took stains out of the most expensive clothing. If someone had a nine-hundred-dollar dress with a spot on it, Uncle Fred was the man they called to take it out. That's all he did. He was a craftsman, a chemist.

But he was not the dandy Aunt Dot tried to make him. She put him in expensive suits, pushed him to act just the right way. But Uncle Fred was a loud talker. He had modified his accent, gotten rid of the Carolina ring, but he was still loud. And if he had a

13

drink, he was even louder. He couldn't help cursing now and then, letting slip a nasty tale or two. He liked to have his fun. Once in a while he'd take me with him when he stopped in at the bar around the corner. He'd have his beer, and I'd stand on a chair and shoot pool. Not exactly the little lady Aunt Dot was grooming. We both had that streak of sassiness, Uncle Fred and me. I guess it's in the Littlejohn blood. And it drove Aunt Dot up a wall.

Manhattan and Queens. That's all I saw of New York. If Aunt Dot knew anything about a place like Harlem, she kept it to herself. To me, the only odd thing about being black was playing Aunt Dot and Uncle Fred's "island" game. Other than that, I never felt different. I had no reason to. There was a movement brewing out there—in the angry streets of Harlem, in the sweltering shantytowns of the South. Brush fires were beginning to crackle, flames that would soon gather into the sixties storm of civil rights and separatism, of Selma and Stokely. But I was untouched. Aunt Dot made sure of that. There was no conflict in her home. No rocking the boat. It was a delicate house of cards she had built, and she wasn't about to see it fall apart. I turned eleven in 1954, the year of *Brown v. Board of Education,* of soldiers on the school steps in Little Rock. That was a big year for the movement. It was a big year for me, too. That was the year I moved back to Virginia.

I don't know why they brought me back. Maybe my father was finally making enough money to pull his family back together.

Aunt Dot and Uncle Fred (1977), with whom Dorothy went to live in New York when she was only two years old. Uncle Fred was Louise's oldest brother.

Maybe I'd become too much for Aunt Dot to handle. There was no discussion, no one sitting me down and telling me, "Now, Dorothy, here's what's happening." That's not how things were done in Aunt Dot's house or in my parents'. To this day, I don't remember the trip down. I guess I was in a state of shock. The resentment, the hurt at being sent away by my own family as a baby, had been inside me for years. My parents never explained why they gave me away. And going back made me resent them even more.

I had been down over the years, for summer visits that never lasted more than a week. I had played with my brothers and sisters—there were finally seven of us then. But I never felt at home, and each time I couldn't wait to get back to Queens, back where I belonged. I hardly remember those visits. Aunt Dot's game had worked better than she could have guessed. But this time there was no return trip. I was in Virginia to stay. No more Wednesday matinees. No more dance lessons. No more of Aunt Dot's delicate dreams.

My family lived in a house now, near a black neighborhood at the edge of town they called Churchland. There were fields around us, and that's where many of the neighbors worked, picking melons, collards and strawberries. My father had left the mill to work in a granary. We lived in a four-bedroom house right on the mill yard. Railroad tracks ran past our front yard, and the train came by twice a day. I remember the engineers who drove those trains—white engineers—throwing candy to us as they went past.

It was strange moving into that house. My brothers and sisters looked at me like I was from another country. The day I arrived I was wearing a little white Peter Pan hat, and I remember them picking at it, touching it like they'd never seen one before. I don't remember my impressions of them. I don't remember how I felt. All I remember is what happened to my things. I came in that door with what must have looked to my brothers and sisters like a world full of things—toys, clothes. And the first thing my brothers did was take my bicycle apart, piece by piece, until there was nothing left. My mother just looked at it, then looked at me and said, "Well, they don't have one."

There were other things my brothers and sisters didn't have.

But my father worked hard to give them what he could. He spent fourteen hours a day at the granary, taking his pay both in money and in feed, which kept us in chickens, turkeys, ducks, geese, goats and hogs. Later, the hogs paid for our first car, a maroon Studebaker.

My mother worked, too, borrowing bus fare from a neighbor and finding a job at a Catholic infant care center—a place whites took their babies for adoption. She wasn't about to work in what she called "white folks' kitchens" for three dollars a week. Instead she left us home and went out each day to take care of those unwanted babies. She was proud of that single white cotton uniform she wore. She washed it every night, kept it spotless and brought home a paycheck of forty-eight dollars a week.

I was a stranger in a strange land, but I made do as best I could. I learned to climb trees and catch lizards, played in the dirt under our house, walked for miles down the tracks, balancing on one rail. I picked wild asparagus and blackberries. I learned to crab. But there was one thing I could never get used to, and that was the praying.

The closest Aunt Dot ever got to religion was reading her *Unity* magazine and mailing off her donation every week. Religion for her was a matter of personal ethics, of codes. Other than the lie she lived, Aunt Dot was as moral, as strict as they come, full of rules and words to live by. She didn't need any church to lay down the law for her.

But in my mother's house, the air was thick with religion—as

17

good and old-time as it gets. Everything was a sin in our house. Playing checkers was a sin, if you did it on Sunday. Cards, rock and roll music—those things were sins any day of the week. And Sunday morning was a day all to itself. It began with breakfast. Food was my mother's way of showing love. If she couldn't provide a lot of material things, she could still feed us. It was a sin to cook on Sunday, of course, so she'd spend all Saturday night cooking. And we'd wake up Sunday to chicken soup for breakfast. I mean, this was soup made with the whole chicken. The feet would be sticking out of that soup, feet with the toenails still on them. We raised those chickens ourselves, then we cooked them, then we ate them.

18

Before breakfast, we prayed. Not a quick prayer at the table, either. This was a session that would shame most churches. Each of us children took a chair from the kitchen and set it up against a living room wall. Mother's chair was across the room, against a wall of its own. We would face the wall, drop to our knees, lean on the chairs and listen to Mother pray. And pray. If she had had a really hard week, it was a really long prayer. And if Momma J was visiting, it was even longer. Momma J was so pious, so perfect, that Mother had to establish that she was just as holy. They'd have a pray-off, and Momma J would go first. She'd pray for the living. She'd pray for the dead. So slowly, with so much feeling. Then my mother would take her turn. She'd pray a little faster than Momma J, but she'd pray longer.

Then Momma J would get happy. She would never shout or

anything—Momma J was too proper for that. She'd just let out a little "Hoooooo. Hoooooo." Like a bird.

Mother would speak in tongues. She could only say one thing in tongues—something that sounded like "Ahh. Pasta. Ahh. Pasta." She'd do that over and over again.

And we would kneel there, shifting from one knee to the other on that hard linoleum floor. Whatever sinning we'd done that week, we paid for on that floor. After the prayer came the Bible verses. We had to memorize them the night before and prove we were ready for church, which came after chicken soup. We were at church two hours. Then we came home and had dinner— chicken dinner.

I never really fit in at home. I talked faster, I walked quicker. My mother told me later she actually would watch my walk and try to imitate it. "That Northern walk," she called it. I'd been to the city, I'd been exposed to things none of my family had ever seen, and that earned a kind of respect from them. Inside that house I was what Aunt Dot was trying to be in New York— special.

But outside, everything was different. Other blacks didn't like me because I was odd. And to the whites, I was just another black, nobody, nothing. In Queens, whites had been my next-door neighbors. The racism there was more subtle, an affair between adults, something kids like me and Maryann never sensed. I didn't know what racial tension was until I met Waldo's kids.

Robert Waldo was the white man who owned the granary. He was the man my father had worked out a deal with for our feed and our garden. Waldo's kids would sometimes come by our house for my mother to look after while their father was at the mill. They were little kids, much younger than I was. But they always called my parents Louise and Grady. These little white kids were talking to my parents the way they talked to me. And my parents let them. Robert Waldo was Mr. Waldo to me and to everybody else. I understood that. Aunt Dot had taught me that adults demand respect from children. She was Mrs. Littlejohn to everybody. Uncle Fred was Mr. Littlejohn. But here were my parents, looking so defenseless, so helpless, so unable to demand anything for themselves or for their children. I couldn't see that they were doing what it took to survive in a Southern town, just as surely as Aunt Dot was doing what it took in New York. All I could do was judge them and tell myself that it could never happen to me. I was different. This was my parents' world, not mine. Mine was back with Aunt Dot.

I didn't have much contact with whites in Churchland. There was a white beer garden across the street where we could go to buy sodas, but we absolutely could not sit there and drink them. Once in a while we would ride a bus with whites on it, but of course we sat in the back. And there was a bus that came through our neighborhood, taking the white kids to their school. We would be waiting for our bus in front of the house, and every single day those kids would come by in theirs and yell "Nigger!" at us. I'd never heard the word before.

20

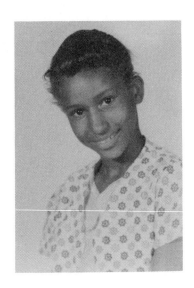

Dorothy at age twelve, after she moved back to Virginia from New York to live with her parents and sisters and brothers.

Neither did I hear much about my relatives. We had an uncle who lived across the harbor in Newport News—Uncle Clinton, a huge dark man with a gold cross stretched across his massive stomach. He'd visit occasionally, but he was the only family member we ever saw besides Momma J. As far as my parents were concerned, there was no family beyond the walls of our house. My mother would talk about Poppa, and here and there she'd mention Aunt Dot's well-to-do parents. But that was it. Like Aunt Dot, my parents had erased the past. I knew why Aunt Dot had done it, but my parents' reasons were not so clear. Slavery was never mentioned around our house. The first time I heard the word, I thought some shame was attached to you if you even uttered it. I told myself it was just another thing about this place that had nothing to do with me. It was some kind of distant stain, something deep in the soul of the South, far re-moved from me and the life I'd lived in New York. When they talked about slavery in school, I was puzzled to think that an entire people could allow themselves to be enslaved—as puzzled as I was to see my parents allow little white children to call them by their first names.

There was a white school about a half-mile from our house, and after *Brown v. Board,* it was integrated—in a manner of speaking. The best and brightest of the black students were invited to enroll. But most parents, including mine, were too afraid of trouble to send us. No one wanted to see soldiers on those steps, so we continued making the thirty-six-mile round trip to our all-black school.

And I continued setting myself apart. One day a history teacher was telling us about the horrors of the antebellum South. What, he asked us, could have been the value of slavery? I raised my hand and suggested, "Maybe the slaves needed that time to adjust to the American way of life."

Another day, another teacher led us in singing the Virginia state song. But he changed the words from "Carry me back to old Virginny," . . . "where this old darkey's heart am longed to go" to "where this old soldier's heart am longed to go." I admired his defiance, but I did not feel his outrage. I was on the outside looking in. This was his shame, not mine.

By the time I began my last year of high school in 1960, the nation was pulsing with change, with a mixture of hope and rage. Rosa Parks had refused to move to the rear of the bus. Martin Luther King had stared them down in Montgomery. And there was a new president in the White House, a man named Kennedy.

But those things were a world away from me. I made no connection between the fact that Rosa Parks said no in Alabama and the fact that I was now able to sit in the front of a bus in Portsmouth. I didn't know who Rosa Parks was. Neither had I heard much of Martin Luther King. My parents were too busy working to pay much attention to the news or to push us to notice. What they knew of civil rights, they kept to themselves. They had a fear of militancy, a fear for their children. Me, I was more interested in starching my crinoline slips, polishing my black-and-white Oxfords, rolling my socks around my ankles, stuffing my bra and biting my lips until they turned purple—my way of getting around Mother's ban against lipstick. There were picket lines in Portsmouth that year, sit-ins at the downtown Woolworth's, but I was more interested in boys than boycotts. And I was still a loner, still setting myself apart. My classmates may have had the movement on their minds. They may have been getting ready to join King and the cause. I wouldn't have known. I couldn't have cared less. I had one friend throughout high school. One. Her parents were in the military. She was not from the South, so she was okay.

I was seventeen when I graduated from high school in 1961. I had taken some tests and done pretty well, well enough to be offered scholarships to two black colleges, but I never gave a thought to going. Those colleges were in the South, and the only thing I had on my mind was leaving. They handed us our diplomas in June, and I was gone, back to New York, to Aunt Dot, to a world that made sense.

Only, it didn't make sense anymore.

I thought Aunt Dot and Uncle Fred would be the same, that I would be able to walk right back into *my* bedroom with *my* furniture. That I'd say I want to go to college, and they'd say "Okay, here's the money." But I'd been gone six years. Maybe Aunt Dot had had too much time on her hands once my room was empty. Maybe money had gotten tight. But Aunt Dot was working now, manning the line at the Ideal toy factory in Queens. I worked there that summer, too, pulling Deputy Dawg dolls out of a stuffing machine and stitching them closed.

That fall I enrolled in night classes at Queens College. I was going to be a psychologist. I worked days as a counter girl at a cleaners, right on the bus route to the school. Roy Wilkins lived across the street from that cleaners. A guy named Gus owned the place—Gus Bass. His joke was "I paid a lot for that 'B.' " Roy Wilkins must have heard that joke every time he came in, and he still laughed each time. Such a gracious man, so dignified, a smile that just jumped out at you. I'll never forget him taking the time to talk to me—me, an eighteen-year-old girl working a cash register, and him the executive secretary of the NAACP. That was the first time I paid attention to an activist group. To me, the NAACP meant Roy Wilkins.

That same year I met a guy in my classes at Queens. He was the first person I'd ever known who was even close to being militant. He was reared in the North, and he was down on whites. He talked about hate, about the Black Muslims. I didn't understand the meaning of all he said, but I liked how he said it. I was, finally, ready for a cause beyond myself.

Over the course of that winter my eyes were forced open. In the South I had felt a cut above, playing the part of the sophisticate, the worldly woman. Now I was surrounded by people who weren't playing games. They talked of Malcolm X, of the Nation of Islam, of the Muslims. They had seen Malcolm X. They knew Muslims. Some of them were Muslims. They dizzied me with their ideas. They stunned me with their passion.

And they took me to Harlem.

I had never been to Harlem. Didn't know what Harlem was. To me, New York blacks were Queens blacks. That was the image I clung to throughout my exile in Virginia. The clean, proper, genteel blackness cultivated by Aunt Dot was the blackness I felt. The Queens blacks I saw when I came back, the kids who had been my friends and were now on their own, were people like Elaine Braithwaite, who went to a fashion institute in France. Or Willie down the block, whose family were Seventh Day Adventists, and to whom being a Seventh Day Adventist himself was still the biggest thing in his life. The people around Aunt Dot and Uncle Fred remained as untouched by the world beyond their neighborhood as my parents were in Churchland. The only thing that had changed in the six years I was gone was that the block was black now. The whites were gone, every one of them. The Jewish doctor still had his office across the street, but he had moved his family the hell out. Still, the blacks in that neighborhood clung to the idea that they were upper-crust. They were Aunt Dot's kind of people. They were islanders in a literal sense, insulated from the world beyond their windows. But the waters around them were rising, especially in Harlem.

I'd never seen anything like Harlem. In Harlem, everybody was angry. Everybody was pissed about something. A movement was alive there. A fire was smoldering. You'd walk into apartments, really huge apartments—you could tell these had been nice places at one time—but they were packed with people now. Angry people. People who were angry at the whites, angry at the blacks, just angry. That's where the voices were shouting. And I listened. There was nothing in Virginia for me. Now there was nothing in Queens either. I was adrift, groping for something to hold onto. But the voices in Harlem scared me. I didn't have the courage it took to commit to the separatism the Muslims preached. I didn't have the hate.

So I joined CORE instead. The Council of Racial Equality. More moderate than the Muslims, this was a group that said we could fight bigotry and still live with whites. We met to discuss jobs, open housing, raising funds for field workers in the South. We picketed the post office. Our outrage was orderly, our defiance dignified. And in the same way Aunt Dot had become an islander, I found through CORE a role I could play—that of an African.

I'd seen the African ambassadors walking in and out of the United Nations building, their clothing so regal, their heads held high. They looked the way I wanted to feel. I'd talked to some Africans and liked the way they discussed American slavery. It was something they said they could hardly understand. It was something to be ashamed of, they said, but the shame they felt was for their American brethren, not themselves. Their words were the same ones I'd spoken to myself in Churchland, lying in bed at night, counting the days until I could leave. The Africans I knew did not talk about their ancestors selling neighboring tribesmen into slavery. This was a fact they conveniently ignored. And of course I was not about to let historical reality interfere with my fantasy. I pictured slave traders invading peaceful villages with clubs and nets, marching their captives off to waiting ships. I identified with those Africans who had escaped the nets, who had kept their dignity intact.

I wanted that dignity. So I made myself African, wetting my hair each night, soaking it in grease, rolling it, sleeping in the rollers, picking it in the morning and patting it down. The ritual took time, but I had my Afro. And I felt good, I felt whole. Until the night my bluff was called.

A friend—a white Jewish friend from my CORE group—asked me to a West African concert. There would be Africans there, real Africans. I was nervous, wondering what to wear. I thought of a line from a Lou Rawls song: "My ancestors were kings of old, they ruled the world and all its gold." Gold. Elegance. I looked at the curtains hanging in my window. White cloth with brilliant green and gold edging. I could see them draping a black queen. With a stitch here and a tuck there, no one would recognize the material being sold in every cheap furniture store in the city. There was even enough for a headdress.

That night, I rode the subway to Greenwich Village, drawing stares all the way, convinced I looked like royalty. I no sooner took a seat at the concert than one of the musicians, a West African, approached and began speaking to me in his native language. It seemed the entire room had stopped to watch. I looked away, hoping he'd disappear. But he went on, pushing closer, uttering sentences I could not comprehend. Finally I shrugged my shoulders, admitting I didn't have a clue. He smiled and moved away. And I sat there, as emotionally naked as a confused nineteen-year-old could feel.

I was not African, but I was black, a fact to be proud of, my Muslim friends reminded me. Not colored. Not Negro. Black. Black was beautiful to the Muslims long before anyone ever heard of Stokely Carmichael. White, they said, was evil. White blood was poison. And that idea made things complicated for me, a light-skinned black. I had the shading of my father's side of the family, and I knew where it came from. There weren't many things my parents told us about their pasts, but one thing my mother had told us tortured me now:

My father's father was white.

Before she married, my father's mother had two children by a white man in Columbia. A man named Norcom. He's dead now, but his children are still around, and they all know their connection to me. Both my father and my father's sister were fathered by that man. Norcom did what he could to help support my grandmother, until she met and married Henry Spruill. Once, Norcom gave her some of his own children's old clothing for my father and his sister. When his wife saw those clothes on two black children, she took my grandmother to court, claiming she had stolen the clothes. My grandmother listened. Then she answered: "I didn't steal them. Your husband gave them to me because these are his children."

It was known, but never talked about. And I did not want to know anymore. I could not bear the idea that I might have white blood inside me. I looked in the mirror at my high cheekbones, my almond eyes, and I decided I was part-Indian. American Indian, another proud race exploited by the white man. That's how I would explain my shading to anyone who asked. Aunt Dot had her islands, and now I had my Indians.

I was still taking classes at Queens when I met Ivan. Ivan Reid. We met on the subway. He was tall, dark and well-to-do—he owned a knitting factory in Brooklyn. He was also fifteen years older than I was, a classic father figure, although I didn't think about that at the time. He was separated from his wife, a separation that lasted until he died in 1985. He never got divorced.

Ivan was from Virginia, too, from Nassawadox, a seacoast town on the eastern shore. But he was a Queens-type black. He didn't have any more to do with his past than I did with mine. And three months after I met him, we were both concerned with something more immediate: I was pregnant.

I quit college and tried staying on with Aunt Dot and Uncle

Fred. But Aunt Dot was unbearable. "Oh, Dotty," she'd moan. "How could you do this?" When I was seven months' pregnant, I moved into an apartment with Ivan. But by that time, he had already become almost irrelevant in my life. Ivan was a wonderful provider. He took care of me, and later the baby. He gave me the lifestyle Aunt Dot and Uncle Fred had given me. But the baby was my focus, the first anchor I had ever felt. She was something of my own, a living, breathing link. On New Year's Eve, 1963, little more than a month after Kennedy was assassinated, the three of us went to a party at Aunt Dot's. When the party ended, I told Ivan I was staying. As simple as that. He thought I was crazy, but that was it. Deborah and I were on our own.

For a time I supported us by baby-sitting. I bought porta-cribs and set up a nursery in the basement of Aunt Dot's house, so I could be with Deborah and still bring in a little money. Then, after a year, I moved to Brooklyn, into a one-bedroom apartment a block from where my older sister, Lethia, lived. Lethia took care of Deborah while I worked, first as a receptionist at Long Island College Hospital, then at an antique shop in Brooklyn Heights. The neighborhood was all cobblestone streets, near the waterfront. The shop was owned by a family of Jews, liberal Jews who wanted a black to work for them. I read every book I could find on antiques, spent eight months there, then came home to Virginia.

I had no choice. Both Lethia and I had sent our babies down

that summer to stay with my sister Lenora in Portsmouth. It was the summer of 1965. When I came down to bring Deborah back to New York, I couldn't do it. Deborah was suddenly surrounded by a family, by aunts and uncles and cousins, by a cushion of warmth I'd never had when I was a child. She was being accepted in a way I never was. There was a wholeness there that the two of us would not have back in that Brooklyn apartment. And there was an opportunity to fill the gaps in Deborah's life that had torn mine apart. I decided then and there we were staying. Deborah was going to have family.

So I was back in the South, the South I had spent my childhood ignoring, my teenage years denying and my young adulthood forgetting. Some things had changed. Most of the "White Only" signs were gone. Massive resistance in the schools had ebbed. There were still incidents, still violence, still racists, but the walls of bigotry were crumbling. The foundations, however, remained. Whites weren't about to step aside easily, especially when it meant giving up jobs. I went to work at Sears Roebuck in Portsmouth that fall as a clerk in housewares. A year later I was a manager of a division, when I applied for a job with the Portsmouth Welfare Department. I called and talked to the director, a white woman who assured me there was a vacancy. When I showed up for the interview, she gulped. She had heard my voice on the phone, and she hadn't expected to see a black woman walk through that door. She didn't hire me, but the welfare office in Chesapeake did. Two years later, I transferred to Portsmouth. And that's where I was working the week "Roots" aired.

I had given Deborah all the family I was able to—my sisters and brothers, their children, my parents. That was all the family I knew. But as we sat and watched Alex Haley's story of generations echoing through centuries, I realized what I had given her wasn't enough. It wasn't enough for Deborah, and it wasn't enough for me. As I watched Haley's family blossom on the screen, I realized there was no running away from the questions that had nagged me throughout my childhood. I was watching one man's story about one man's family. My own story had yet to be told. There was so much I did not know, so much to ask.

The day after the series ended, I'd found a how-to genealogy book in the paperback rack at the grocery store. It said you start with yourself, so that's what I'd done. I took a pencil, a notebook, even colored pens, and drew pages of diagrams of the Churchland mill yard, of the house we lived in, of the hog pen, even of the trees on our street. I colored the trees green. I wanted so badly to make my thin past come alive, and colored pens were all I had.

But my memories stopped at the mill yard. I hardly recalled Columbia. We didn't get the Studebaker until I was in high school, and then we'd only drive down to North Carolina maybe once a year. All I remembered of my parents' hometown were dusty lanes, cousins whose names I hardly knew, Momma J's attic, the pecan tree in her front yard—the hugest pecan tree I ever saw—and a cripple named Ben, who dragged himself down the street on his knees. Whenever somebody mentioned Columbia, I'd see Ben.

Ten years earlier I could not have walked into my parents' house with the questions I brought that winter morning. I was still too unsure then—unsure what I thought of them, what they thought of me, what I thought of myself. The resentment of my childhood still lingered. So did the confusion of my years in New York, the years just before Deborah's birth. But I'd come a long way. For a single black woman in 1977, I was making it. I had a good job, earning fifteen thousand dollars a year. I had my own house. I had what all the books coming out at the time were calling self-esteem.

And I still had my eyes on Africa. I was no longer wearing drapes, but I had the same need to belong there. Haley had traced himself back to the continent. I would, too. That's why I went to my mother, not my father. His line led to a white man, but my mother's line, as far as I knew, was pure. Her people were all very tall, very dark. They could take me all the way home.

Grady Spruill—that was my father's name. He never had had a lot of hair, but by now he was bald as an egg. Strong. Slender. His body worn hard and lean by work. And my mother, Louise Littlejohn Spruill. She grew up slim, got heavy during her child-raising years, and was now small again as she wiped her hands on a kitchen towel and sat down to talk.

I didn't know what to expect. The questions I'd had as a child

33

I'd kept to myself, making up my own answers. Guessing. Imagining hidden shame and shadowy guilt. I assumed that my parents' silence stemmed from some secret sorrow—all somehow
linked to slavery and the South. I thought I knew the answers, so
I never asked the questions.

Now, for the first time in my life, I was asking, and it was as if
I'd loosed a rainstorm. My mother's eagerness, her pride and
the details of her memory washed over me, sweeping me into
another time, into a place peopled by men and women I had
never met. She could have taken me there twenty years earlier if
I'd only asked. But I wasn't ready then. I was ready now. Her first
story led to another, and the next to one after that. Neither of us
knew it that morning, but this was the first step of what would
become a ten-year journey.

"OVER DE RIVER"

She began, of course, with Poppa—James Ed Littlejohn, her father. Through my mother's eyes, he was a saint. She knew hardly a thing about how or where he had grown up. He wasn't from Columbia. He was from the fields and farms to the west, what folks in town called "over de river."

"Over de river." Alligator, Gum Neck, Creswell. Places they called towns, and they still do. But they were no more than one street each then, maybe a half-mile long, with houses on both sides. Mere rest stops along the dirt roads that wound through the Carolina countryside.

Farm folks lived out there. If they didn't want to work in the fields, they came in to Columbia. That's why James Ed Littlejohn came. He worked in the log woods, and one morning in 1903 he rode into town, atop a wagon full of timber. He was twenty-four, a lean, tall, sinewy man. And as he drove past one of the larger houses on the town's main street, he noticed a girl sitting on the shaded front porch. A dainty thing, dignified, wearing a cool summer dress, long black hair combed down her back just so. She was only thirteen but she was the finest-looking woman he had ever seen.

Her name was Jechonias Jenkins, granddaughter of the Reverend Ed Jenkins—"Pappy" Jenkins to most of the folks in town. Pappy Jenkins' people had come from the western end of the state. He wasn't a Columbia person either. But he was a good businessman. He owned a wagon, and made good money hauling logs for blacks and whites alike. He bought some land right there in town and built a little row of houses he rented out to loggers or migrant workers. They called that stretch of town Jenkins Row. He built a church, too, one of three in town. Then he found ten people to come on Sunday and became a minister. Just like that. A Disciple of Christ minister. But he was always a businessman first.

Pappy Jenkins and his wife Alethia—the family called her Momma Letha—had one child. But that one child was plenty enough: Louisianna Jenkins. Fiery, flashy, with a mind of her own. And spoiled like no other child in town. Pappy Jenkins had more money than he knew what to do with, so he gave Louisianna whatever she asked for. And she asked for plenty, all her life. As a girl, she had the run of that seven-room house they lived in. As a woman, she had furs, silk dresses, shoes. When she died, she had a gold ring on every finger.

She was the daughter of a minister, but that didn't stop Louisianna from becoming the first black woman in Columbia to get a divorce. At first, she wouldn't get married. She wouldn't marry Octavius Brickhouse, the man who fathered both her children—Jechonias and a son named Setan. The Brickhouses were a solid, decent family, and Octavius was an Army veteran—he had pictures of himself wearing a World War I soldier's uniform. But Louisianna didn't want any part of marrying him. It was no scandal to have children outside marriage then. It hadn't been long since all these families had been living on plantations, where plenty of children were born with unmarried parents.

Momma Lou wouldn't marry Octavius Brickhouse, but she did marry a man named Noah Sutton. She liked to travel, to get out of Columbia and visit bigger cities like Norfolk. That's where she met Noah Sutton. She brought him back to Columbia for all—including Octavius—to see, and married him. She stayed with him a few months, then got tired of him. So she got divorced. As simple as that. The judge tried to talk her out of it, but Momma Lou always got what she wanted.

She wasn't much for marriage, and she wasn't much for raising children. She was too busy. She was always away in Norfolk or New York. Buying clothes. And furniture, which she shipped back home on the same trains that came to Columbia for timber. Louisianna sent home plenty of gifts, but she didn't spend much time there herself.

It was Pappy Jenkins and Momma Letha who raised Louisianna's children. And they treated those children the same way they treated Louisianna. They had enough money to hire people to do all the work around the house. What chores they didn't hire out, Momma Letha took care of. Jechonias Jenkins was not reared to clean house, to cook, to do anything with her hands but brush her hair. Brush her hair and sit on the porch on hot summer afternoons, which is where she was the day Poppa first saw her.

Poppa might not have had a chance with Reverend Jenkins' granddaughter if Momma Letha hadn't known his people. But she was born "over de river" herself. She was a Spruill. So that was in Poppa's favor. And Jechonias—Miss J then, Momma J later—was taken with the tall, dark man who came calling that Sunday afternoon.

The courtship was a family affair. Poppa came only on Sundays, sitting in the parlor with Miss J, Pappy and Momma Letha. The young couple were never alone, and Poppa always left before the kerosene lamps were lit for the evening. It took a year, but finally Pappy Jenkins signed the papers that allowed his fourteen-year-old granddaughter to marry Mr. Littlejohn, the logger.

Poppa and Momma J had four children—three boys and Louise, my mother, born in 1907. But it was really as if Poppa had five children. Momma J was used to being taken care of, and things didn't change just because she was married. Poppa picked up where Pappy Jenkins and Momma Letha left off. He was the one who cleaned house, cooked the biscuits, pressed the clothes, bathed the children at night and got them up in the morning before he left for work. Momma J, she just glided through her days, rising late and cooking breakfast at her own pace. About ten o'clock every morning, the school would let my mother and her brothers run home and eat the breakfast Momma J had finally prepared. Yes, Poppa had himself a house full of prima donnas. If my mother hadn't had me and my sisters and brothers, she would have become another Momma Lou or Momma J. But having seven kids gets that prissiness out of the system quick.

Poppa didn't mind it though. He kept his family happy. He even gave Momma J a house as nice as the one she'd grown up in. A white doctor from "over town"—across the tracks—sold Poppa a house, a beautiful house. Seven rooms. Gingerbread trim. Porches on the front and back. All Poppa had to do was move it across the railroad tracks, which, with the help of half the town, he did. That house was thirty-five feet tall and thirty feet wide around the sides, and they moved it in one piece. Hoisted it up with jacks and set it on massive wooden dollies. Wrapped it with chains and cables. Hitched a crew of mules to the front. Then they inched it down the sandy street, stopping every ten feet to set planks under the logs. Up and over the tracks. Around two corners to Poppa's plot, where he had a solid brick foundation waiting.

Momma J did the rest, filling her new parlor with fine Victorian furniture, fitting an organ into a corner. These were things

Dorothy's grandfather, James Ed Littlejohn—Poppa—as a young man.

her grandparents had given her. And Momma Lou. Unless company was coming, that furniture stayed draped in white sheets, to keep the street dust and sunlight off the velvet.

This was the house my mother grew up in, the house my parents lived in when they were married. It was the house my mother lived in when I was born, the house she left behind when she joined my father in Virginia, the house with the attic I remembered from my childhood visits. But as my mother described it now, it was new to me, as was everything else I was hearing.

There were more rooms than they needed in that house. During potato season, the spare bedroom was always filled with a family of migrant workers. The town hotel was for whites only, so come harvest time, the black pickers found lodging wherever they could. And Poppa was eager to help out.

Poppa was a righteous man, even more God-fearing than the Reverend Jenkins. When the family got together at the Jenkins

Poppa, Louise's father, was a member of the first generation in his family born free.

house for Christmas, Pappy would always have some wine around. And he liked to slip a sip to the children. Mother remembered how when she was a little girl Pappy would give her a little wine. And she remembered how Poppa would frown. He'd put up with it, but he didn't like it. There was no alcohol in James Ed Littlejohn's house.

Mother had no idea where Poppa's righteousness came from. He wasn't so much religious as just right-living. He worked hard, in the log woods and later in the sawmill. He never drank. Never used profanity. And he was tolerant beyond reason. Tolerant of his kids. Tolerant of his wife. Tolerant of everyone else in town. He was the most reasonable man around, and because of that, no one wanted to disappoint him. When my father, Grady, was a younger man, he'd not only drink, but he'd gamble, too. In a little town like Columbia, you did both right on the street corner, right in public. But if he and his friends saw Poppa coming, they'd quick whisper to one another, "Here comes Mr.

Littlejohn." And everybody would straighten up, hide the bottles, put the dice back in his pocket. If somebody was staggering, Poppa would say, "Don't you think you boys ought to help so and so get home?" He wouldn't criticize. He wasn't pious. And that made him even more respected.

Pappy Jenkins. Momma Letha. Momma Lou. They were all just names to me before. Hollow ghosts. But as my mother spoke that day and all the days that followed, the names became people, they took shape. The town that was nothing but a word to me came alive through the richness of my mother's memories. I could smell the sweetness as she described yards rimmed with thick honeysuckle. I could see the men drifting home from work in groups of twos and threes as the sinking sun threw shadows across the dirt streets and the twinkle of kerosene lamps appeared in upstairs windows. I could hear the voices floating on the evening air as adults sat on their front porches, gossiping and watching the children play.

But even mother's memory had its limits. I was searching for dates and relations, links between names, ancestral lines that would lead me back through centuries, to my beginnings, to Africa. I had my genealogy book in my pocket, and I was following the rules, digging for hard numbers. But Mother didn't think that way. These were people to her, not limbs on a family tree. Each person was different. Each was a story. And that's what my mother gave me. Stories.

When she referred to Priscilla Rowsome, it wasn't as Momma

Letha's half-brother's daughter. It was as Cousin Priscilla, the
town witch. Mother remembered how on weekends, wagons
would line up a block long in front of Priscilla's house, waiting
for her to work her magic. She was a root doctor, gathering
herbs in the woods and fields around town and turning them
into powders and potions. She had the cure for whatever ailed
you. She was different, and she looked it. She always wore a wig,
a flaming red wig. And her clothes were stuffed with pillows—
her stockings were stuffed, her hips, her behind, her chest. She
was a walking marshmallow. Mother always said as a child that
she wanted to be around when Cousin Priscilla died so she could
finally see just what was underneath all that padding.

But it wasn't just her shape that set Priscilla apart. She was
also the only black woman in town who had a white boyfriend.
Everybody called him Old Man Pritchett. He came across the
tracks to eat all his meals with her, and he gave her gifts. Her
smokehouse was filled with hams Pritchett gave her at slaughter
time. It was illegal for blacks and whites to have a relationship,
and beyond that, Pritchett's white relatives were embarrassed
and irritated by the whole thing. But no one could touch Priscilla. More than once the sheriff issued a warrant for her arrest,
but she just ignored those pieces of paper. She never did go to
court. When she died in 1950, all Pritchett's family could do was
march straight to her smokehouse and get back what hams were
still there.

I always imagined life in those days in that town as dismal.

They had no plumbing. Water was collected in rain barrels set out in the yards. There was no electricity. No trash collection. Poppa had to dig holes in the yard to bury whatever garbage he couldn't burn. Medicine was primitive or nonexistent. There was a shack at the end of town, and if you got tuberculosis, that's where you went, to be away from everyone else and to die. Poppa wasn't the only one to die of typhoid in 1944. His brother Medicus had a daughter Malvina, who died of typhoid that year, too. It was an epidemic, and all the town could do was wait for it to run its course, the same way they'd watch a fire burn itself out in the woods. There was no use fighting it. Just let it do its damage, and pick up from there.

44

But the quality of life in that town had nothing to do with comfort. Today, there are three thousand people in Columbia, white and black. Back then, there was a fraction of that number. Even less when Mother was a child. And almost everyone was related. Everyone had a place. No matter what you did, you were never an outcast. Maybe Momma Lou was wild. Maybe Cousin Priscilla was a witch. But they were still part of the family, still part of the town. They still belonged.

Those first days with Mother I spent hours listening to her stories and jotting down details, names, dates, places. Together, we were peeling back the topmost layer of our family history, probing the generation above hers, a generation I'd never known, except for Momma J. The names were familiar, but the specifics of these lives were new. Still, they were all Columbia people. I could connect to Columbia. As little as I remembered, I had still been there, walked those streets, sat on some of those porches.

But then Mother began mentioning names I'd never heard before. Names from beyond Columbia. Dickson. Hortin. Honeyblue. Cabarrus. Baum. Phelps. No one in Columbia had these names. They were from "over de river." From Poppa's past.

I'd never heard these names as a child because my parents never talked about them. They were a world away, not part of my parents' lives. They lived around Creswell, only ten miles from Columbia. But when my mother was a child, ten miles was no small distance. Especially those ten miles. The road was dirt, of course, with woods and swamp on both sides. The last mile of that road actually went into what they called Piney Swamp. There, the hard dirt turned to soft muck. Two-by-fours were laid side by side the length of that last stretch, to hold the weight of what traffic there was. After a good rain, you couldn't tell road from swamp.

There were no lights, and even on the clearest night the moonlight couldn't penetrate the canopy of trees that hung over that road. So you had to make it from Columbia to Creswell and back before sundown. Or you spent the night. A trip like that wasn't easy in a horse and buggy, and most families in Columbia didn't even have that. Momma J used to tell Mother about the "over de river" relatives arriving in Columbia in wagons on a

45

Columbia, North Carolina, c. 1900.

Saturday afternoon, parking in front of Pappy Jenkins house and getting fed by Momma Letha. They were Momma Letha's kinfolk. But those visits were few and far between. And the links between the families crumbled away over the years. Someone would die in Creswell, and word wouldn't reach Columbia until the funeral was long past. A baby would be born, and the announcement might not cross the river for weeks. By the time my mother was a little girl, Creswell was a mystery to her, another place altogether.

One of the few things that brought the two towns together was baseball. Baseball was big in Columbia. Come Sunday afternoon, Bibles were laid aside and everyone would head to the

Columbia, North Carolina, c. 1920.

ballfield. Mother remembered the boat coming in from Elizabeth City, with a band on it and a baseball team. That boat would come down the Albemarle Sound, up the Scuppernong to Columbia, and by the time it unloaded, the whole black section of town would be over at the baseball diamond, waiting to watch the Columbia Tigers take on the out-of-town team. When the Tigers had an away game, they'd pile into Poppa's boat, the same boat he used to fish lost logs out of the river. That boat seated twenty, and Poppa would steer, taking the team up to Elizabeth City, down to Creswell or over to any of the other half dozen towns that made up that loose league. Up until my father left town, he played third base on that Columbia team. Even after I was grown, he used to talk about the Tigers, brag about how they "never, *never*" lost a game.

My mother went along on one or two of those boat rides. But what she knew of Creswell, she remembered from the trips with her aunt Lizzie.

Aunt Lizzie—Elizabeth Brickhouse Swain. She was my mother's great-aunt, from over in Creswell. She was "Lizzie Brickus" to everyone, even after she married William Swain. Everyone knew about Swain and his temper. Everyone knew how he beat Aunt Lizzie, too. When he died, Aunt Lizzie dressed him up just as pretty as she could, then she put him in the ground just as happy as she could be, humming and singing the whole time. She wasn't singing any sad hymns either. My mother asked her once why she didn't cry at that funeral, and Aunt Lizzie just smiled and said, "Noooo, honey. If I'd a cried, I'd a been sassin' God."

After Swain died, Lizzie moved to Columbia, into Poppa's house. She was right at home there, hosting neighbors out on the porch and enforcing her own code of conduct. She didn't like gossip, but she'd hear plenty of it out on that porch. She'd just sit quietly and listen to the stories. Then, if she didn't like what she was hearing, she'd glance toward the sky, take a deep breath through her nose and pronounce, "You know, when it rains down from heaven, everything just smells pure and sweet, just smells cleeeean." Then she'd pause and look back down. "But piss just stinks."

48

Aunt Lizzie would take my mother with her when she went back home to visit Creswell. She didn't go often, and when she did, it was by train. There were two passenger cars on the logging train, but the seats were expensive. Not too many people took that ride, and it was a rare treat when Mother went with Lizzie. That's how Mother learned what she knows about Creswell. Aunt Lizzie would dress her up and show her around. Mother remembered being shown to Martha Dickson. And to Odessa Cabarrus. The names were there, deep in her mind, but they hadn't been pulled out in years. She was breaking ground that hadn't been touched for decades. For weeks it went like that, one "over de river" name leading to another. Then one day my mother mentioned a name that meant more to me than any of the others.

Alfred Littlejohn.

Poppa's father. My great-grandfather on the Littlejohn side. Pappy Jenkins' generation. Mother had never mentioned Alfred because she knew him even less than she knew the Creswell people. He died in 1925. He was from Creswell, but about the time Poppa married Momma J, Alfred Littlejohn moved north, across the Albemarle Sound, to Edenton. That was a fifty-mile trip in those days, long before there was an Albemarle Sound Bridge. If Creswell was a world away, Edenton was in another universe.

In Edenton, Alfred became a tenant farmer. His first wife had died—Poppa's mother—and he'd married again. He had another whole family in Edenton, boys who were Poppa's half-brothers. One summer when they were young, Mother's brothers—Uncle Jim and Uncle Fred, yes, Aunt Dot's Uncle Fred—went to spend a summer with one of Alfred's Edenton sons, a man named Johnson Walter Littlejohn. Johnson owned more than a hundred acres of prime farmland, and he took his work seriously. When Jim and Fred arrived—Momma J's pampered little boys—the first thing Johnson did was hand them some tools and point them to the fields. Those two boys—my uncles—came home to Columbia early that summer. And they never went back to Edenton.

Mother didn't remember much about Alfred except that he was black, very black. On his marriage license, which I found years later, the county clerk wrote "dark" in the space for color. As my mother spoke, I could feel my blood rushing. I could see the fingers pointing to Africa.

Each night, I brought home a handful of notebook pages on which I'd scribbled the details of my mother's stories. I would read them over, rewriting them, sifting out names, dates and places. Then I did just what my pocket genealogy guide told me to do: I went to the federal census records in the library.

I hadn't spent much time in libraries before. I hadn't had the time or the need. But beginning that winter, and for the next four years, the downtown Norfolk Public Library became my second home. Copies of federal censuses for seven central Atlantic states, including North Carolina, were stored there. Any

50

Johnson Walter Littlejohn, Poppa's half-brother from Edenton.

American in search of his family history can work his way through the censuses, decade by decade, back to 1790, the year of the first one.

Any American, that is, except a black one. For most blacks on the census trail, there is virtually no data before 1870. Free blacks, if they were the head of a household, can be found on censuses taken earlier than that year. But slaves were listed merely as property. Their names do not appear on any census taken prior to the end of the Civil War. They exist on those records only as numbers. If a white man owned ten slaves, that number was entered under the property column on the census form.

Still, I had the 1870, 1880 and 1900 censuses to work with. On these, we were people. The 1890 census records for virtually the entire country were destroyed in a fire in Washington, D.C., in 1929. That's a gap every genealogist learns to live with.

Genealogist. The word sounded so authoritative, so scientific. But I would soon find out this paper chase was no science. There was nothing precise about the beginnings of my search, no formulas that would lead me directly to the information I was after. If I was going to find the pieces I needed to fit my puzzle, it was going to take logic, guesswork, persistence. And luck.

The Sargent Memorial Room of the Norfolk Public Library's main branch is upstairs. Glass-walled. Bright. Fluorescent lights. The focus of its sixteen thousand books and thirty-six hundred rolls of microfilm is Norfolk and Virginia history. Old city newspapers, magazines, directories, maps, photos, school yearbooks, court records, marriage and death certificates, deed books, wills, county histories, even old postcards are stored in the room's file cabinets and on its shelves. But I wasn't after those things the day I first walked in. All I wanted were the censuses.

Before "Roots," I would have drawn some looks walking into that room. The very titles of the books on those shelves told you who they were written for:

Virginia Daughters of the American Revolution.

Lineage Book of the Daughters of the American Colonists.

Lineage Book of the National Society of Daughters of Founders of Patriots of America.

The General Society of Mayflower Descendants.

First American Jewish Families.

Scots in the Carolinas.

The Lees of Virginia.

The Byrds of Virginia.

Gentlemen of Virginia.

Blacks had little business in there. But after "Roots," everybody was looking for his or her family history. I was not the only black in that room the day I first walked in. But I was the only one who kept coming back. Wednesday nights. Saturdays. Lunch breaks from work. Before long, the librarians knew me by name.

That first spring, I arrived armed with a core of "over de river" names, sifted from my mother's memories: Baum, Brickhouse, Cabarrus, Honeyblue, Hortin, Phelps and Littlejohn. These were Poppa Littlejohn's line, the parents, aunts and uncles my mother remembered. My genealogy book told me to begin with myself and work backward. My mother had taken me as far as she could go. Now I had seven names to search for in the 1900 census, the most recent census available, since, according to law, these records must be seventy-five years old before they are made public. By the time I finished searching ten years later, the 1910 census was also opened.

The censuses were filed by state and year, then by county, then by townships or cities within each county. The families my mother talked about were scattered throughout the countryside. She hardly remembered the names of many of the people, much less the names of the places where they lived. So I focused on three counties: Tyrrell, which included Columbia; Washington, which included Creswell; and Chowan, which included Edenton.

Through the glare of the microfilm machine I traced the

53

house-to-house march of the census-takers who walked through the nineteenth-century Carolina countryside. Names were not arranged alphabetically or by family, but in the order in which they were gathered. Neighbors would appear next to one another on the form. I could imagine the census-taker knocking on one door, then the next, although I had no idea how far apart those doors were. They could have been next-door neighbors who chatted across the side fence, or two farmers separated by acres of land.

Next to each name were columns for age, sex, color, occupation, value of real estate and property, birthplace, education, ability to read and write, eligibility to vote, even a column marked "deaf and dumb, blind, insane, or idiotic." Each census-taker wrote out the information in longhand script, some more legibly than others.

Because Mother was so unsure about the names of the actual towns her father's relatives had lived in, I searched the entire records of each county, page by page, looking for the surnames I knew. And I found them, some in towns my mother had never mentioned. Cherry. Cool Spring. Sunny Side. I had no idea if these places still existed, but they were out there, somewhere, in 1900. And so were the names I was after. Three Cabarrus families. Four Honeyblues. Seven Baums. I found Daniel Hortin, Cousin Odessa's grandfather. But there was a Herbert Hortin, too. I located five Littlejohn families, but none listed Grandpa Alfred's name in the household. I had no idea which of these families were my kin and which were not, so I copied every entry bearing any of the names I knew.

But other names pushed their way in as well. I discovered Collinses listed in Honeyblue households, Bennetts and Vaughns living with Brickhouses. Families were sharing homes. Which might be related to me? I couldn't know, so I took them all down. The names were mushrooming before my eyes, faster than I could keep up with them. I could have limited myself to the Littlejohn track, tried to trace the straight and narrow path, but that was no longer all I was after. I was after my family history now, not just my own. And the only way I could deal with so many names, so many unknowns, was to throw away my genealogy guide and make my own rules. I knew our movement was restricted by the legal system before the Civil War, and by economic reasons afterward. These restrictions dictated who our family members would be. Since historians already determined that in 1870 my ancestors, who had been slaves, would still be on the land they lived on as slaves, I would go to the 1870 census and work forward.

What a difference. In 1870, I could find only one Baum family. One Cabarrus. I found seven Littlejohns, but this time Grandpa Alfred was among them. The oldest man in my mother's memory, and there he was. Twenty-three years old. His brother Peter, who had gone with him to Edenton, was two. Mother's great-aunt Judy—Judith Littlejohn Honeyblue—was four. And above the names of these children were their parents, Fred and

Lettice Littlejohn. Two names beyond my mother's memory. I had peeled back a layer even my mother had never seen.

Fred Littlejohn, born 1816—a slave.

Alfred Littlejohn, born 1847—a slave.

What I had denied as a child, refused to think about as a woman, was now staring me in the face. Of course it was no surprise. Where else could I have come from? Where else could almost every black I'd ever known have come from? Still, the reality of the names scrawled before my eyes, names written in ink that had been dry more than a century, hit me in my heart. This was no classroom discussion, no CORE group debate, no protest slogan. "Before I'd be a slave, I'd be buried in my grave." I'd sung that line, marching for my civil rights. Now I felt so arrogant. So smug. It was easy for me to sing about a choice I never had to make. But here were people who had lived the life I chanted about. People with my blood in them.

And I realized how close I really was to their lives. Poppa, my grandfather, was born in 1879—a member of the first generation of his family born free. My mother, Louise, born in 1907, was among the second. And I was of the third. Suddenly the past seemed so near, so immediate. Here I had assumed such a distance from my parents' world, from the lives they had lived. And now, suddenly, in a very real, very personal sense, time was squeezed, the generations were pushed together. It was only yesterday that my people were slaves. I knew then, for the first time, that my search was going to take me beyond freedom, back into a time even my mother knew nothing about.

The 1870 census now looked different to me. It was no longer a beginning point, any more than 1900 was. Yes, I needed those specific names my mother had given me. But I had no idea how those names might be connected to the other names on those census pages. And they could be. So I took them all down, the name of every black person on every page of the 1870 census for those three counties. Then I did the same for 1880. And for 1900. First, there were dozens of names. Then hundreds. Then thousands, copied one by one into my growing stacks of note-books. I could look at only so many pages at a time before my eyes gave way. Then I'd go home, then to work, then back to the library again. Days passed, then months, and eventually years.

My friends were interested at first. Then, as time passed, their interest turned to amusement. Then they became merely polite. And finally they just told me to leave them alone. I had one friend who, every time I talked about it, would say, "I'm sick of them damn slaves." Even your best friends will put up with an obsession for only so long. Then they just don't want to hear any more about it.

But my relatives, they couldn't hear enough. All of them, that is, except Aunt Dot. I saw her once or twice over those first few years, and each time she would take me aside and ask me, "Why? Why are you doing all this, Dorothy? No one needs to bother with all this. What is the point?" Aunt Dot never changed.

In May of 1977 Carlton Littlejohn died, and I went to Edenton for his funeral. He was one of Johnson Littlejohn's thirteen children, one of Alfred Littlejohn's forty grandchildren. Forty.

57

This was my first chance to meet some of the people my mother had told me about.

There was the funeral, then the feast, then another feast at the house of Carlton's brother, Calvin. There must have been sixty people at Calvin's house, most of them family. Cousins from New York I had never seen before, cousins from North Carolina I'd never seen before. They were Mother's generation. We talked. And we went back to the cemetery, where dozens of Littlejohns were buried. I had never seen or heard the names on most of those stones.

Ruth Littlejohn, born 1925, died 1941. A teenager.

George Littlejohn, born 1899, died 1899. An infant.

There was one Littlejohn buried there that nobody at the funeral knew. Daniel Littlejohn, born 1845, died 1930.

And there were names everyone knew:

Johnson Littlejohn, born 1886, died 1946.

Alfred Littlejohn, born 1847, died 1925.

More names. More dates. They all went into my notebooks. They all became part of my frame of reference, pieces around the border of an intricate jigsaw puzzle. I also got a sense of the land my people had lived and worked on, the land Alfred's son Johnson had bought.

A month later I interviewed Momma J. She was eighty-seven, living in a rest home in Columbia. That home didn't have more than five beds in it, and hers looked across the street to where her and Poppa's house had stood, the house they had brought

Jechonias Jenkins—Momma J—and Poppa, in front of their Columbia, North Carolina, home, c. 1940. Many of the houses in town were vine-covered like this one.

across the tracks from the white side of town. It was long gone by now, torn down.

Her hair was not as long anymore. It was on her shoulders now. It was silver, but she still wanted it to be black. She was still vain. She had a black wig she didn't wear much, but when she died, my mother put that wig on her. She said Momma J would have had a fit if she'd lain in that casket with that gray hair.

I went to see Momma J that June day, but I had waited too long. She wasn't senile, but she was frail. There was so much she didn't remember. She hardly remembered her son Dorris, the one of my mother's three brothers who did not live into adulthood. He died when he was sixteen. Everyone said it was "jumpin' pneumonia" that killed him. Who knows what it really was?

Momma J didn't have much to say that afternoon, but she did say she still talked to Poppa sometimes. And she called him her "old man." It sounded so strange to hear that phrase, street talk coming out of Momma J's proper mouth.

Seven months later, in January of 1978, Momma J died. And all she knew died with her.

An urgency crept over me then. My family is a long-lived lot. But they were dying now. With Momma J gone, my parents' generation was the oldest left in my direct line. Time began to seem of the essence.

A month after Momma J's funeral, I was at the library. I was working on the 1880 census by then. Over the year since I'd begun my study, whenever I needed a break from the microfilm machine I would browse through the stacks of books at the rear of the room. They were genealogy books, the histories of white families. I had first come to those books as outlines, models that I hoped would show me how to write my own chronicle. The books were full of details, fascinating facts. Schools attended, land and buildings owned, positions of prestige attained, all neatly packaged between hard covers. Compared with the bits and pieces of my own history I was scrambling to collect, these books seemed so final, like the Bible. But as I read more and more of them, I noticed something was wrong.

First, every family descended from European nobility. Not just from Europe, but from nobility. Those who couldn't find royal connections through legitimate lines claimed relationships through illegitimacy. I was amused, but it was painfully familiar, this groping search for legitimacy. I had been there.

But even more obvious than their need to connect to Old World thrones was these white families' distortion of their New World wealth. Rarely were slaves mentioned in any of these books. These were Southern families—wealthy families whose well-being depended on the strength of black shoulders. But blacks were mentioned only occasionally in these pages, and then it was as a "house servant" or a "cook." These white people had rewritten their own histories, the same way Aunt Dot had remade hers. They were shifting facts to fit their situation, to create the image they wanted, to put on the face they needed, just as I had done as a young woman. Apparently blacks weren't the only ones weighed down with antebellum baggage.

But I kept reading these accounts, because there was more I needed from them than form or even facts. I had assumed that each time a slave shifted hands from one owner to another, his name was changed to the new owner's. What I was looking for as I drifted through these white genealogies was one of the names of my own family. To trace my line into slavery, I would have to find the white connections. Finally, in February of 1978, a month after Momma J's funeral and a year after I watched "Roots," I found a name.

The Littlejohn family of Edenton, North Carolina. White Littlejohns in the same county where Grandpa Alfred settled. Their story was buried in a four-volume collection of genealogical magazines everyone in the library called *Hathaway's*. By now these chronicles all looked the same to me. But this one I read with a purpose.

William Alexander Littlejohn had arrived in Edenton from Inverness, Scotland, around 1760. He became a shipping merchant, married Sarah Blount, fathered fourteen children, attended St. Paul's Episcopal Church and died at age seventy-seven. The line and lives of his descendants were detailed over the book's next twelve pages. Names, birthdates, houses and land owned, dates of death. But no mention of slaves. Not one.

I took the book across the room with me to the microfilm reader, found the 1790 census for Edenton Township, Chowan County, and there he was. William A. Littlejohn. In the property column next to his name was marked the number of slaves owned: Sixty-two.

William Littlejohn was the third-largest slaveholder in Edenton in 1790. In doing their family history, the Littlejohns had done away with the history of the families they owned. On one side of the room were leather-bound lies, and not fifteen feet away sat the truth.

Now, besides charting every black in those three counties from 1870 forward, I was also after the white side of the picture: White Baums, white Cabarruses, white Brickhouses. Everything I'd read and heard convinced me that a black's name depended on the name of his owner and that names changed as often as owners. The slave narratives I would later read gave that impression. Booker T. Washington said the same thing. Everybody assumed that this constant shifting of owner-dependent names was virtual law.

But over the course of the next two years, I began to doubt it. In the same 1870 census in which I found black Littlejohns, Cabarruses and Baums, I could find no whites with those names. Neither were they on the 1860 lists. In 1790 I found plenty of white Cabarruses and Littlejohns in Chowan County. But the white Cabarruses had disappeared by 1820. There was only one white Littlejohn in 1840, none in 1850. Yet slavery continued until 1865, so who owned the slaves with these names after the whites with these names were gone? And why weren't the slaves' names changed?

I didn't know where to go. The rules were falling apart, and I didn't know how to replace them. I kept doing the only thing I could depend on: scanning the post-antebellum censuses for black names and linking those names from census to census, charting the growth of the families. By the time I was back to the 1900 census, more than three years had passed. I now had a sense of the Littlejohns scattered across the landscape—how they were related, where they had come from, how they had moved. The floor of my den was ankle-deep in post-antebellum family trees.

The search absorbed my life. But it hardly touched Deborah's. She was happy I was happy, but she had her own kind of discovering to do. High school is a complex, confusing time for any teenager. For a black teen, it is even more critical. Deborah went to an integrated school, and this was the 1970s, but several incidents told us little had changed since I was her age.

In eighth grade, she was one of two blacks in her school assigned to an advanced science class. Within a week the white teacher convinced the other black student he'd be "happier" in a lower-level class. Deborah resisted the same offer. Her junior year in high school she was outraged when her classmates held a "Slave Day" to raise money. White students came to school with whips and chains and bid on servants. Deborah wrote a letter to the local newspaper, asking how Jewish students might feel if a "Hitler Day" were held. And her senior year, when Deborah applied to the University of Virginia, her guidance counselor reminded her that no black from Churchland High had ever gone to U.Va., that even if she were accepted, she might get "frustrated" competing against all the "really bright" students there.

Deborah was accepted at U.Va. in the spring of 1981. She left for Charlottesville that fall. It had been four years since I had first talked with my mother, four years of virtually living in that public library room. My mother had given me all she had to offer. So had the library. I was finished with the censuses, and there were no more records for me there. Still, there were questions.

Where were the white families with my family's surnames?

Where did my great-great-grandfather Fred come from?

Was he African?

Fred Littlejohn was property. To find him, I would have to go to the courthouses in Washington, Tyrrell and Chowan counties.

That's where they kept the bills of sale.

THE
ROAD HOME

It's the kind of road that makes the South the South.

Two lanes of blacktop weaving in and out of towns the interstates left behind. Between the towns, dirt fields and distant treelines. Mailboxes with no house in sight. A tractor crawling down the right lane, its overalled driver blind to the traffic backed up behind him. Billboards in cornfields. Heat mirages shimmering off the asphalt. A blue-shirted road gang hacking weeds while a shotgun-toting guard rests in the shade.

That's Route 17, the road that took me from Portsmouth to Edenton. It's a fifty-mile trip, but I marked it by minutes, not miles. I made that drive so many times I can almost count the mileage markers in my mind. And each trip began with The Dismal, three minutes from my driveway.

The Great Dismal Swamp. On a clear day, workers up on the cranes at Portsmouth's Naval Shipyard can look north to the skyline of Norfolk, west to the farmland of Suffolk and east to the suburbs of Virginia Beach. Progress in every direction. But when they look south, they see The Dismal, looming on the horizon like a low-lying greenish-brown cloud. A quarter-million acres of muck stretching into North Carolina. People have tried to tame that bog for centuries, but no one's ever done it. William Byrd knew it couldn't be done. Byrd was a Virginia plantation owner who explored the swamp while charting the state line back in 1728, the year he wrote this description of the colonial jungle his men led him through:

"The Dismal," as he named it, "is foul with damps that corrupt the air and render it unfit for respiration, nor do birds fly over it, for the fear of noisome exhalations that rise from this vast body of dirt and nastiness."

It covered more than half a million acres back then. There has always been lumber in there, along with tar, pitch and turpentine, things that meant a lot to settlers. But it was impossible to get anything out through the thick low-hanging trees and shallow water. George Washington tried in 1763, gathering partners to buy a forty-thousand-acre piece of the swamp and drain it. But he gave up. Maybe the snakes scared him away—three of the only four species of poisonous snakes found in America are found in The Dismal Swamp. Every now and then one drops off a tree branch into a fisherman's boat.

Still, people who live around The Dismal insist its water alone is worth a trip in. It's foul-looking stuff, brown and foamy, laced with tannic acid from the juniper trees. But Indians and colonists believed this "juniper water" was as good as medicine, and farmers still feed it every once in a while to their sick animals. There was talk years back about building a health resort beside Lake Drummond, deep at the center of the swamp. But the only hotel that's ever made a go of it in The Dismal was a place they called the Half-Way House, located right on the Virginia-Carolina line. They say it was a rowdy place, with more than one drunken argument settled by a pistol duel—arranged so the loser and winner stood in different states, making it so hard for the law to sort out the jurisdictions that no one tried. In later years, Norfolk sailors would run down there with their sweethearts to get married under the lax North Carolina marriage laws. At least that's what people say. The Half-Way House is long gone.

But more than anything else, The Dismal Swamp has always been a place to hide. During Prohibition, moonshiners brewed whiskey deep in its forests. Earlier than that, runaway slaves hid in the shadows of the swamp, living hermits' lives. Some of those slaves came from Carolina, from the same direction my search took me.

I'd think about that as I drove down Route 17 in the summer of 1981 and all the seasons that followed. I'd look at the waters of the canal running alongside the road—it's part of the Intracoastal Waterway now, but they just called it the Swamp Canal when it was dug in the early 1800s to connect the Albemarle Sound to Norfolk—and I'd imagine white men poling their boats in that stillness, peering into the dark swamp, hunting for their runaway property.

Fifteen minutes and I'd be across the state line, still in the swamp. Eight more minutes and it was the town of South Mills, where the road crosses the canal and bends southwest, leaving The Dismal behind. The Waterway Motel. Charlie Boy's Cigarettes. A few trailers and tin-roofed houses. That's South Mills. That, and the gas station where Daddy used to stop and get us popsicles on our childhood trips down to Columbia.

Beyond South Mills, it was open countryside, all furrowed fields and scraggly pines. A turnoff to Morgans Corner. Then, Elizabeth City, a place that, like so many Southern towns, has to look backward for a luster it lost long ago. In colonial times, this was an important seaport, perched on the Pasquotank River, which spills into the Albemarle Sound, which runs to the Atlantic. In 1677, nearly a century before the Boston Tea Party, the settlers here staged their own protest against the British, a little revolt they called "Culpeper's Rebellion." The town's cotton and timber mills boomed in the 1800s, thanks to the deepening and widening of the Swamp Canal. But once paved roads were built out along the Atlantic coast, ships no longer needed to come up the sound to Elizabeth City. The mills slowed down, and the waterfront was left to pleasure boats. Today, the drive through town takes you past the brick carcass of a closed cotton mill, past a Ford dealer, past BoBud's nightclub and Ron E's Pizza and a Zip Mart. There is a sign for the College of the Albemarle, for Roanoke Bible College and for Elizabeth City State University, which was Elizabeth City State Teachers College when I was a girl. That was where many of the best black students went. But after integration, the cream was skimmed away and the school skidded into mediocrity. For me, Elizabeth City meant a seventy-five-cent cup of ice cream at the Tastee-Freez. Then back on the road.

On past Hertford, home of Jim Hunter. Hunter was the pride of Perquimans County when he was pitching baseballs in the big leagues. The newspapers called him "Catfish" then, but he's always been Jimmy to the folks in Hertford. Now Jimmy Hunter is back home, farming.

Eight minutes beyond Hertford is the turnoff to the Albemarle Sound Bridge. We'd take the bridge on our family trips to Columbia. But I skipped that turn now, staying on 17 into Edenton, driving past the houses and fields east of town. This is where Grandpa Alfred's son Johnson bought his land, land Johnson's sons still farm, although lately the government's been paying them more to leave it alone than they can make growing anything on it.

Finally, Edenton, the seat of Chowan County.

I'd been there before 1981—at funerals like Carlton's. But I'd always spent those visits on the family land, outside town. Now I was in white Edenton, where tourists take waterfront horse-and-buggy rides down oak-shaded streets, past houses that date back to the Revolution. The homes are huge, dwarfing anything in Columbia. The brochures describe Queen Anne, Federal, Georgian and Jacobean architecture. There are pillars, porches and gazebos. Urns and fountains sprout from manicured yards. Small, tasteful signs are planted in each lawn, noting the pedigree of the address: "James Iredell House—1800"; "Joseph Hewes House—1765"; "Alison House—Pre-Rev." The main street slopes down toward the old wharf area and ends at the water, where a cannon and a statue of a soldier face the town, their backs to the sound. The base of the statue is inscribed: "Our Confederate Dead, 1861–1865."

Three blocks east of that monument, across the railroad tracks, is the black part of town. There are no statues there, no historic markers, no walking tours or open houses. The homes are small, wood-framed, with tar paper and tin on the roofs. There are no sidewalks. This is Edenton's backyard, but by now I knew it was all linked—the weary black homes, the opulent white ones, the ships that once crowded that waterfront and the plantations that still sit in the countryside. There was no indication in the brochures I picked up at Edenton's visitors' center that blacks ever even lived here. But by now I knew better than to believe someone else's history.

The brochures make much of the fact that this was the first capital of North Carolina, that the pirate Blackbeard ducked in during his terrorizing of the coast, that a member of the first U.S. Supreme Court was from Edenton, as well as signers of the Declaration of Independence and the Constitution. All bright-side stuff. No mention of the dark side of Edenton observed by John Brickell, an Irish doctor who visited the port in 1730 and published his *Natural History of North Carolina* in 1737. In that book, Brickell described how important slaves were to Chowan County's planters, how "Negroes" were too valuable to be bought with mere paper money, how it took gold or silver to buy a "Black." He also detailed the differences between slaves brought directly from Africa and those born in America. The latter, he noted, were raised as Christians and seemed better behaved, more obedient. The Africans, on the other hand, were defiant, according to Brickell, who wrote, "I have frequently seen them whipt to that degree that large pieces of their Skin have been hanging down their Backs, yet I never observed one of them to shed a Tear. . . ."

On the surrounding plantations, where he saw them living in "convenient Houses," Brickell wrote that some slaves were tempted to flee into the surrounding swamps. But most were less afraid of their white masters than of the Indians who still lived close to Edenton and who, wrote Brickell, "have such a natural aversion to Blacks, that they commonly shoot them when ever they find them. . . ."

By the time of the Revolution, Edenton was a busy seaport, unloading ships fresh from the West Indies and filling the holds

73

of those bound for New England. Between 1771 and 1776, according to port records, 827 ships berthed at the town's wharves. A history published by Edenton's Chamber of Commerce describes the products shipped in and out during that five-year period:

> Local farmers and merchants exported almost ten million staves, more than sixteen million shingles, 320,000 bushels of corn, 100,000 barrels of tar and a great variety of produce. There were 24,000 barrels of fish, along with 6,000 hogsheads of tobacco and about a thousand deerskins. The greatest imports were rum (250,000 gallons), molasses (100,000 gallons), sugar (600,000 pounds), salt (150,000 pounds), and linen (400,000 yards).

No slaves are mentioned. But slaves were there.

74

By 1790, according to the history, Edenton was a town of about one hundred and fifty homes.

> Her population of 1,600 included about 1,000 Negro slaves. There was wealth but it was not well distributed, even among the whites. About a third of the white residents owned no slaves at all while the five great slave-owners, Cullen Pollock, Nathaniel Allen, Josiah Collins, Samuel Dickinson, and William Littlejohn owned almost half the town's Negro population.

William Littlejohn. Even before I got to the courthouse, I found scraps of the Littlejohn legacy in Edenton. In the cemetery of St. Paul's Episcopal Church—the church mentioned in the family's genealogy—there was a weathered, moss-covered gravestone inscribed with the name Mary Littlejohn. She was born in 1813, and died a year later. I found no other Littlejohn

graves, but two blocks toward the waterfront I found the Littlejohn house. The sign on its lawn dated it 1790. Whitewashed,
two stories, it wasn't nearly as spectacular as some of its neighbors. But the Littlejohns were a prominent family in eighteenth-
century Edenton. A guidebook to the homes of the town notes
that Sarah Blount Littlejohn, William's wife, was one of fifty-one
women who signed a resolution in 1774 vowing not to drink tea
imported from England. Today a teapot is Edenton's official
logo, stamped on stationery and postcards. The guidebook also
noted that on a summer day in 1791 Sarah and William Littlejohn sat on the front lawn of their home and witnessed a tragedy
detailed in the June 10 edition of that year's Edenton *Gazette:*

> On Friday afternoon last a most melancholy accident happened
> here . . . A small party, among whom were . . . Miss Fanny
> Gray, Miss Sally Littlejohn and Miss Jane Littlejohn, having pro-
> posed to sail in the harbour in a whale-boat, just after they left the
> wharf . . . struck upon one of the sunken wrecks, when the boat
> bilged, immediately filled with water . . . and . . . sunk to the
> bottom . . . Miss Gray and Miss S. Littlejohn were saved, but,
> alas! Miss Jane was missing . . . it was upwards of 20 minutes
> before the body was found . . . conveyed to her father's house
> (only about 200 yards distant) . . . every endeavor for her recov-
> ery, but in vain. She was in the 17th year of her age. Her funeral
> was attended the next day . . .

This was the family I began with in the courthouse records.
Two hardbound, burgundy-shaded indexes the size of old-fash-
ioned atlases listed all property transactions made in Chowan
County prior to 1878. Each book was more than four hundred

pages thick, and each page listed, in loose alphabetical order, the names of people involved in transactions and where each transaction could be found among the dozens of property deed books filed on the room's shelves.

The deed books were even more tedious than the censuses I had lived with in Norfolk. Written in Old English longhand script were page upon page of legalese. Whereas after whereas. Parties of the first, second and third parts. Property "bargained, sold and confirmed" was then "conveyed, assigned and delivered" to "said" and "before mentioned" people. It took me an hour to read through one transaction. Six of them and I called it a day, climbed back in my Toyota, drove home to Virginia and began arranging my next day off from work. Those leave days were rarely less than a month apart.

But it didn't take me long to find William Littlejohn. He was not only all over those deed books, but his name also appeared regularly in newspaper notices of the time. According to some of those notices, William Littlejohn ran one of the busier general stores in town:

"The Subscriber has on Hand, About 1600 Bushels of exceeding good Cadiz Salt . . . William Littlejohn. Edenton, Feb. 26, 1793."

"William Littlejohn, Has for Sale, at his Store, Old Apple Brandy . . . Raisins, molasses . . . dry goods . . . Edenton, Jan. 1, 1794."

"The subscriber has for sale, a quantity of Peruvian Bark . . . very lately imported from Cadiz . . . to accommodate families that may be in want of that most useful and necessary medicine. William Littlejohn. Edenton, July 19, 1796."

"The subscriber has just imported from New York . . . a general assortment of Dry Goods . . . and has also furnished his store at the wharf, with . . . Grocery and Ship Chandlery Goods, which he intends continuing in future, as a Grocery and Ship Chandlery Store, Entirely. William Littlejohn. Edenton, October 24, 1796."

Apparently, William Littlejohn had done well for himself since sailing from Scotland around 1760 at age twenty. His marriage to Sarah Blount didn't hurt. Her grandfather was a Captain James Blount of the Virginia Blounts, whose property in the Edenton area included two sizable plantations, several wharfs and waterfront lots, a tannery, a fishery and a bank that later became the State Bank of North Carolina. When Littlejohn married her in 1771, he not only received her dowry, but was in line to share what she inherited when her father died four years later.

Slaves had to have been part of all these dealings. I knew William Littlejohn owned sixty-two slaves in 1790. The census records back in Virginia had told me that. Two references in the Edenton *Gazette* notices also linked Littlejohn to slaves:

Chowan County, Whereas complaint hath this day been made to us, all Justices of the Peace . . . county aforesaid, by Joseph Blount, Esq. of said county, that certain slaves, viz. Brutus, belonging to John Byrne, Robin, belonging to a Mr. Taylor, Aaron, belonging to John Blount, Pompey, belonging to James Beasley, and sundry other slaves . . . have absented themselves from their masters service and are now in arms, and are committing many acts of felony in the said county, to the great terror of the good people thereof . . . And we do hereby, by virtue of an act of the Assembly . . . declare, if the said slaves do not surrender themselves and return home immediately after the publication of these presents, that any person may kill and destroy the said slaves . . . without accusation . . . of any crime . . . 16 March 1793. Samuel Dickinson, Nathaniel Allen, William Littlejohn . . .

Ten Dollars Reward. Run away from the subscriber, on the 7th of April last, an old stout negro fellow named Dick Pepper, a caulker by trade . . . He had been run away from November, 1793, till the above date, when I fell in with him . . . on Ballard's Bridge; upon seizing him he knocked down my servant and endeavored to get me down, in the presence of one Solomon Elliott . . . I bought him November 1793, from William Littlejohn . . . George Mackenzy, Edenton, July 4th, 1798.

But the property deed books did not list slaves in any of Littlejohn's transactions. All they showed were land purchases and sales, and legal transfers. I checked the limited port records kept at the visitors' center, but I could find only two vessels listed to William Littlejohn, and neither made trips to Africa or the West Indies.

Where did his slaves come from? Sarah Blount must have brought some when she married Littlejohn. But I could find no records of that. Some may have been bought in Virginia or South Carolina, two states known for their established, first-class slave markets. But I had no way of checking this either.

So I checked Littlejohn's children. Fourteen were born, but only four were living when William Littlejohn was thrown from a horse and buggy and killed in 1817. Three of those children had moved away by then. Only the youngest, John Wilson Littlejohn, was still in Chowan County.

John Littlejohn was hardly mentioned in the family genealogy. There was his birthdate—March 12, 1786. But no death date. Scant mention of his wife and nine children, five who died young. No achievements. Reading those pages, it seemed as if John Littlejohn never lived.

But the Chowan County property books showed otherwise. When his father died, John took power of attorney for both his brothers, who had moved away. I couldn't find the details of how William's estate was divided, but almost all that John inherited was gone within ten years.

On June 17, 1826, John Littlejohn signed a Deed of Trust with the State Bank of North Carolina's Edenton branch. He owed the bank six thousand and forty-five dollars on two notes and the guardians of two estates twenty-five hundred dollars. For those debts, he put up most of the Littlejohn family property: several lots in downtown Edenton; a wharf; warehouses; a water lot on the sound; a one-hundred-and-forty-acre plantation adjacent to a plantation owned by a man named Josiah Collins; and—I held my breath as I came to the names—twenty-three slaves:

> . . . to wit, Jack Bissell, Charles, Tom Evans, Edmund, Peter, Soloman, Jane and her son Ben, Pleasant, Daphne and her son Ned, Jack, Peter Blount, Mingo, Fortune, Bob, Dick, Cato, Amarillis, Charlotte and her two children Joe and Dillale, and Teresa.

My family. I knew they were there, among those names. And there were more. On June 26, just nine days after his deal with the bank, John Littlejohn registered a bill of sale to Josiah Collins, the man mentioned in the bank deed, one of the town's biggest slave-owners. No buildings or land were involved in this transaction. No, this time the sale was strictly for slaves. For six thousand dollars, Littlejohn sold Collins "thirty-two negro slaves." Less than two hundred dollars a person. And this time the paper listed more than just names:

> A negro woman named Celia aged about thirty six years together with her five children: negro Fanny aged about thirteen years, negro girl Kate aged about eight years, negro girl Peggy aged about six years, negro Milly aged about two years, and negro boy Isaac aged about three months; negro woman named Sylvia aged about thirty four years, together with her six children: negro boy Nelson aged about fourteen, negro boy Tom aged about twelve years, negro girl Carolina aged about eight years, negro girl Ann aged about six years, negro boy Granville aged about three years and negro boy Hamilton aged about two; negro woman named Elsy aged about thirty years, together with her six children: negro girl Amy aged about ten years, negro boy Fred aged about eight years, negro girl Mary aged about seven, negro boy Peter aged about five years, negro boy Jacob aged about two years and negro boy John aged about two months; mulatto woman named Teany aged about thirty years together with her four children: negro girl Penny aged about twelve years, negro girl Priscilla aged about nine years, negro boy John aged about seven years and negro boy Daniel aged about four years; negro woman named Patricia aged about thirty four years together with her two children: negro girl Eliza, aged about eleven years, and negro girl Catharine aged about ten years; negro woman named Sal aged about twenty four years, together with her two children: mulatto girl Carolina aged about eight years and negro Heather aged about one year: and negro girl Lavinia aged about fifteen years.

Women, children and babies. John Littlejohn had been allowed to keep possession of the slaves he deeded to the bank. He needed the men's muscle, so he only mortgaged them. But these women and children he sold outright to his next-door neighbor, Collins. And among them was "negro boy Fred aged about eight years." The 1870 census had listed my great-great-grandfather Fred's birthdate as 1816. This bill of sale placed his birth at "about" 1818. This Fred had brothers and sisters named Amy, Mary, Peter, Jacob and John. Great-grandpa Alfred's youngest brother was named Peter. Alfred's half-brother Alpheus had children named Amy, Mary, Peter and John. Both my mother and my grandfather had sons named Fred.

It had to be.

That eight-year-old slave was Fred Littlejohn, Alfred's father. The woman named Elsy was my great-great-great-grandmother, my ancestral mother. I carried her blood. If I was right, I was now seven generations deep into my family. I was into the eighteenth century.

I had to know what became of Elsy and her children. But I also had to stay with John Littlejohn's story. If what I'd heard of slave-naming customs were true, Elsy and her family became Collinses. Only the slaves Littlejohn kept would keep his name and lead me to mine.

Following John Littlejohn's name through those property books was like watching a man tumble down a hillside. In 1828 he sold four slaves for two hundred dollars apiece. He was scrambling now, desperate. In 1829 and 1830, he sold more lots in Edenton and repaid some of his debt to the bank. A temporary foothold. Then, in 1840, he was in the hole again, this time for almost seven thousand dollars to an Augustus Moore, more

81

than a thousand to a William Roscoe and seven hundred and eighty dollars to a John Jones. I don't know what Littlejohn's problem was, whether he was a gambler or just a bad businessman, but year by year he was signing away the fortunes his father had made.

On the 1840 Deed of Trust John Littlejohn put up as collateral his stock of mules, cattle, sheep and hogs, "farming utensils of every kind and description," all the household and kitchen furniture, silver, glass and crockery ware, and those twenty-three male slaves. He was given six months to pay the debts or he would lose everything at public auction, including the slaves.

And that's where the records stopped. I could find no trace of John Littlejohn after that 1840 deed. I don't know if he paid those debts. I don't know when he died. I do know that his son, William A. Littlejohn, was saddled with at least some of his father's debts. In 1841, according to the property books, William Littlejohn commissioned a sale of his one-hundred-and-forty-acre family plantation, along with everything else his father had put up in the 1826 and much of the 1840 Deed of Trust with the bank. Everything, that is, except the slaves. They weren't mentioned. By 1842 all the Littlejohn holdings in Chowan County had been liquidated. The trail of Littlejohn's property and, more importantly to me, of his male slaves had run out. Eight years later, according to the 1850 census, William Littlejohn owned nothing and was living in a room at the Bond Inn in Edenton.

For me, that was the end of the Littlejohn line. On paper, that family's slaves were gone. Now it was time to follow Elsy and her children, time to begin again with yet another name—Josiah Collins.

It was the winter of 1981 now. Deborah was away at college, and I was alone. I had made the trip to Edenton about ten times by then. In the cold, with the trees bare and the fields hard, the drive was even lonelier than usual. The streets of Edenton were empty now, the tourists gone for the winter and the chill winds off the water driving everyone else inside. But the courthouse was still open, and its books were full of Collinses—Collinses and slaves.

My search of the Norfolk census records had prepared me. In 1790, Josiah Collins owned thirty slaves. I also noticed the business firm of Collins, Allen and Dickinson, also known as the Lake Company, owned one hundred and thirteen slaves in Edenton that year and one hundred and thirteen more in Tyrrell County—which then included what later became Washington County—"over de river."

On the 1800 census, Josiah Collins listed forty slaves in Edenton. He and his partners also listed a hundred and forty in Tyrrell.

In 1810, Josiah Collins had a hundred and forty slaves of his own in Edenton and another hundred in Washington County. No partners were mentioned.

I found the Collins name in will books as well as property

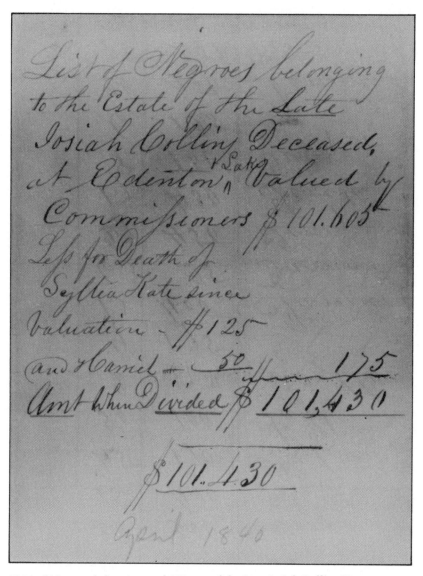

"List of Negroes belonging to the Estate of the Late Josiah Collins II at Edenton"...(1840).

A List of Negroes at Edenton belonging to the Estate of the
Late Josiah Collins Esqr Valued by Commissioners April 1st 1840

Name	Age	Value	Name	Age	Value
Alick Caughten	33	350	John Taylor (Sailor)	42	500
Aaron (Disabled Shoulder)	54	10	Jerry Granberry	57	150
Alfred	3	100	Jim	2	75
Alfred Page	19	550	Joe Bartlett	10	300
Alfred	8	200	Jeffry	5	125
Alick Creecy	49	350	Jack Emmons	50	200
Austin	36	650	Jacob Summer	48	250
Alick	15	500	Josiah Bartlett	40	450
Alick King	13	400	John Creecy	23	700
			Julius Caesar (Inflammation)	18	500
Briley	16	550	Jim	12	550
			John Willy	13	400
Cooper	47	275	Joshua	56	175
Cyrus (very weakly & sickly)	16	350	Jerry		with mother
Charles (Ship Carpenter & caulker)	49	500			
			King (just blind & helpless)	13	00
Daniel (very ordinary)	18	500	Kit	79	00
Dave	10	300			
Daniel	3	100	Lewis (Carpenter)	47	600
Dicks	8	200			
Dave Granberry (Carpenter)	50	300	Moses Murdaugh	43	350
Dick & Cooking	71	00	Miley Tamah	10	300
Dave Murdaugh	19	700	Mily	1	with mother
			Milly	3	100
Edwards	15	550	Miles	46	275
			Melvin	22	700
George Jones	45	300			
Granville (Back poorly & sickly)	19	500	Ned Caughten (Shoemaker)	55	200
George Bartlett	48	350	Nelson	38	700
			Ned Cohely (Infirm Hernia)	59	50
Hamilton	15	550	Ned Taylor (sore eyes)	55	25
Henry	11	325			
Hardem	1	with mother	Providence	11	325
Henry	3	100	Prince	13	350
Harry	1	175	Peter	55	150
Isaac Blackburn	67	00	Dinough	9	250
Isaac	16	550			
			Randal		960
Jackson	14	550			857.50
Job	10	300			
Joshua	1	with mother			
John Roberts		with mother			
		10935			

85

Continued

Name	Age	Value	Name		Age	Value
Solomon	15	$300	Uriug	(Shoemaker)	15	$700
Simon	44	300				
Stephen Nefow	16	275	William		5	125
Solomon	19	700	Washington		46	275
Long Stephen (Infirm debulils)	48	00	Wallace		22	700
Solomon	2 mos	with Mother	Washington		16	500
Spencer	6 mos	with Mother	William		12	350
			William		6 mos	with Mother
Tom	26	700				$2,650
Old Tom	79	00				4,425
Tom (berry Ordinary)	12	300				8,750
Tony Wilcomr	59	175				10,925
Thompson	21	700				
Thompson	21	700		Sum Total Males		$26,750
Tom	13	375				
		$4,125				

Continued Females

Name	Age	Value	Name	Age	Value
Amy Graneburg	53	$75	Dillah	67	00
Adeline	24	450			
Amy	43	150	Elizabeth	9	175
Amy Wood	13	300	Esther	11	225
Ann	20	450	Emily	12	250
			Eliza (& child Nanny) 2 dy	25	570
Becky Jones (Weaver)	49	150	Emily	18	450
Barbara	52	100			
Bonetta	13	300	Fanny Satton	26	450
Betty Miller	80	00	Fanny (& 2 children Celia & Betty)	26	550
Becky	14	350			
Betty	11	225	Harriet	13	300
Betty	7 mos	with Mother	Hannah Paine	52	100
Caroline (& children Teresa & Hester)	21	550	Harriet	11	225
Chloe Pratt	56	100	Harriet	2	with Mother
Charity (and child Jerry)	41	300	Hester	6 mos	with Mother
Charlotte	2	50			
Calista	21	450	Jenny & Britton	12	250
Cora	16	400	Jenny	65	00
Celia	49	135	Joanna	13	with Moth.
Caroline	32	450			
Catharine (& child Spencer)	23	500	Kate (and child Solomon 1 3o)	22	500
Celia	2	with Mother			$3,975
		$5,475			

Name	Age	Value	Name	Age	Value
Lettuce and child (Milly)	39	350	Reba	3	75
Lucinda	41	75	Rachael	4	100
Lavinia (1 child Dorian)	29	500	Rose (hopelessly Blind & usless)	13	11
Lucy	29	450			
			Scotty (and child Jeannette)	36	400
Mary	12	250	Sally	10	200
Maria	36	350	Sally Ann	10	200
Molly	38	300	Susan	19	450
Margaret	15	400	Sylla Kate	47	125
Molly	45	170	Sylvia Patience	47	130
Minna	50	100	Salt	37	335
Mary	9	with mother	Scythia	9	200
Maria	9	175			
Maria	13	400	Tamar (and infant Jeanette)	39	350
Mary Ann	63	25	Tamar	14	350
Myrtilla	27	450	Tiney	43	170
Mary Ann	17	450	Teresa		with mother
Milly	8	150	Tiney	6 mo	with mother
Malvinia	6	125			
Marinda	20	450	Venus Haughton	22	450
Mary Creecy	18	450	Venus (1 child Mary 2 m)	34	500
Martha Mills	18	450	Venus (hopelessly Blind & usles)	14	80
Martha Haughton	16	400	Violet	52	100
Marguerite Standing		with mother			$1,741.15
Milly	16	400			11,170
Maria	6	125			3,975
Molly	13	300			5,475
Maria	10	200			
Murriah	10	200	Sum Total Female		$24,765
Murriah	58	50	" Male		$26,750
					$51,515
Rachel (1 child William 8 m)	21	500	Mrs Blounts		
Nanny (Deranged & Infirm)	42	00	Hannibal	45	300
Nelly	5	100	Sonny	38	250
Nancy	15	400	Mustapher	24	700
Nancy	2	with mother	Maxwell	22	700
			Charlotte	13	300
			Alfred	9	250
Peg	64	25	Fanny	7	150
Penny 1 child Landson	36	400	Augustus	2	} 125
Phillis (seamstress)	48	200	Emily (twins)	2	} 125
Prissa	9	175			$5,129.
Patience	2	75			
Peggy (1 child Marguerite Standing)	19	500			
Penny 1 children Harriet 2 & Teney 3 m	25	550			
Prisilla (1 child John Roberts)	22	500			
		$11,170			

books. The family patriarch, Josiah I, died in 1819, leaving "all the land between Washington and Tyrrell counties and 100 negroes" to his grandson, Josiah III. It was Josiah II who bought John Littlejohn's slaves in 1826, and he died a widower in 1839, dividing his slaves equally among his children. So it was Josiah III who eventually ended up with most of the family's land and slaves.

So many slaves. From so many places. The Collinses bought some of their slaves at Edenton estate sales. Others were bought in Tyrrell County. Some were purchased as far away as Virginia. Except for the Littlejohn purchase, most of the Collins slaves were bought only a few at a time: A total of twelve in 1786, four the year after that, two in 1788. Most of the slaves listed on the deeds and bills of sale were mothers and children. Few single men. A family of eleven was bought in 1793, and another of thirteen in 1795. Both those sales included men, but these were fathers. It seemed that Collins preferred buying a man if the man had a family. A slave was less likely to run away if he had his wife and children with him. There were more effective, more efficient ways to control a slave than with whips and chains. Apparently the Collinses knew that.

The censuses bore this out. In 1800 there were a hundred and forty slaves on the Collins plantation, but only three white overseers. In 1810 the ratio was one hundred to two. What I had heard and read all my life about slave families broken apart by their masters was apparently not always true. At least not with the Collinses.

With every discovery I made came more questions, and the one that nagged me most as I read the Collins records was the disappearance of partners' names in the 1810 census and the subsequent jump in the number of Collins slaves. I had a pretty good idea of what had happened, but I didn't find proof until the spring of 1983. That's when I opened a deed book to the 1803 breakup of the Lake Company.

The elder Josiah Collins had indeed become a partner with Nathaniel Allen and Samuel Dickinson in 1784. They called their firm the Lake Company. Now, in 1803, the partnership was dissolving. And among the ten-page inventory of company holdings were two pages that took my breath away.

They were titled "A List of the Negroes at Lake Phelps, belonging to Misters Collins, Allen and Dickinson, 10th November 1803."

It wasn't just the names and ages of one hundred and fourteen slaves that stunned me. Or that among them were sixteen mothers with children. Sixteen identifiable families. Suck and her two sons born before 1800. Donkey and her twin daughters born in 1789. It was the African names. Slaves brought from Africa? There were African-sounding names on the list: Quaminy, Cuff, Tass, Cag, Eggy, Abijac.

There were Serena and Patrina as well—Spanish names.

And Bridgette—French.

Jericho, Hannah, David, Adam and Soloman—biblical.

Even these all made sense, since slave ships often dropped their cargoes off in the West Indies for "seasoning" on the sugar plantations. Those who survived arrived at the auction blocks with island-born children bearing Spanish and French names, as well as Christian ones.

But it was the African-sounding names that obsessed me. Suddenly, it wasn't just my Littlejohn bloodline I was seeking. It was all the names on the list—especially the ones that sounded African. I needed to know which were actually African. I needed to know where they came from. I wanted the names of countries, of tribes.

The published history by the town's Chamber of Commerce noted that a cargo of Africans was delivered to Edenton after the Revolutionary War:

90

> A visitor in 1786 was in town in June when the brig *Guineaman* arrived from Africa with a hundred Negroes in her hold. All were between 20 and 25 years of age, were "extremely black, with elegant white teeth," and spoke "a most curious lingo. . . ." The group had been purchased by the firm of Collins, Allen and Dickinson for an immense project these men were planning. They meant to employ the Negroes in digging canals to drain Lake Phelps in Tyrrell county and thereby gain access to an enormous tract of virgin timber.

But that helped me little. The best answers I could get came from a College of William and Mary anthropology professor named Eric Ayisi.

Ayisi recognized some of the names as West African—most slave traders at that time took their cargo from the Gold and Windward coasts of the continent. Along those coasts and inland, the slaves could have come from anywhere within a four-hundred-mile region. He told me I'd have to find the name of a ship and its log if I wanted to get any more specific.

As we talked about the names, Ayisi began telling me about his own family. His father was a Ghanaian chief, and Ayisi himself had been raised in the family's tribal compound. His father had five wives, but Ayisi's mother was the first wife, the only one who didn't live with him in his compound. Each week the chief took turns with a different wife, coming to her home, where she would cook for him and share her bed with him. Ayisi said there were never any conflicts among the women, except when the chief occasionally slipped away to visit one wife during another's week.

I wondered if my Africans had multiple wives. One male slave could have been the husband of several wives and the father of many children, if he were still following the customs of his African family. I had to find out more about the African slaves who were brought to Washington County.

I went back to the port records, this time looking for Collins' ships. Those papers showed four sloops belonging to Josiah Collins. They sailed to St. Croix, Turks Island, Norfolk and Haiti. No voyages to Africa. Maybe the slaves had come from Africa to the Indies, where Collins bought them. But I had no way of finding this out.

I studied my 1870 census lists, hoping some of the African names would be there. They weren't. Had they all died? Why weren't their names passed on to their children? I didn't know where to turn.

Then I saw the brochure. It had been there all the time, among the dozens of tourist pamphlets in the visitors' center. Who knows why I picked it up after walking past it so many times on my way to the port records? But there it was.

"Somerset Place: Splendid Nineteenth Century Coastal Plantation Estate . . ."

". . . home of the Josiah Collins family . . ."

". . . A North Carolina Historic Site . . ."

". . . Visitors Are Welcome."

THE
ARRIVAL

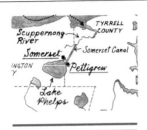

T he sun beat down hard the day I drove to Somerset. It glistened off the glassy surface of Albemarle Sound as I crossed the four-mile bridge to the south side and passed through Skinnersville, a sandy stop in the road known for its juke joint and its homemade whiskey. Moonshine. Daddy used to say runners from as far away as Virginia would make the trip down here just to pick up some of that Skinnersville corn. It didn't look like much had changed since we were a family on our way to Columbia. The juke joint was still open, and out in those woods, out there somewhere, they were still making liquor.

A few miles on and I passed the state prison. Daddy used to toot his horn at the convicts out in that dirt exercise yard, and they'd wave, just like we were somebody they knew. I always liked that. But this day the yard was empty. The heat had driven the prisoners inside. Sunlight flashed off the concertina wire coiled at the tops of the fences. The only person in sight was a lone guard perched at the top of a brick tower. He was letting down a rope with an empty lunch bucket tied to the end. Somebody would be by later to pick it up.

This is the road to the coast, to Cape Hatteras and Nags Head. It's sixty miles from here to the Atlantic, but already the streetside stores in the one-light towns have suntan lotion and towels in the windows. When I slowed at the west end of Creswell, I saw a sign in a supermarket window: "Why Pay Beach Prices?" Looking at the dirt parking lots, the scorched brown grass, the silos off at the edge of the fields outside town, the beach seemed a world away.

94

There's not much to Creswell—Miss Donnie's Restaurant, Triple E Auto Sales, Spear's Hardware, Alexander's Bargain Barn. Dogs sleeping in doorways. Faces behind windows. Things move slowly around a place like this, and on a hot summer day they don't move at all. There's a lot that doesn't move in a place like Creswell. The day I turned toward Somerset, there was a flag draped in the window of a diner owned by the town's deputy sheriff—a Confederate flag.

I'd never taken this turn before. I had never needed to. We always passed through Creswell on our family trips, but we always went east toward Columbia. Now I was headed south into swampland I'd never seen. Green marsh and black water pushed at both sides of the raised roadway. I thought of the dirt road from Columbia to Creswell my mother had told me about.

I came to a bridge crossing a dark, silent river. It was maybe twenty feet wide here, with trees jutting from the mud banks, leaning out and shading the sluggish, scum-coated water. Insects danced over the surface, hovering in the heat. This was the Scuppernong River. And this was Spruill's Bridge, the spot where Poppa Littlejohn would unload the baseball team back when they'd come to play Creswell. The bridge was wooden then. It's concrete and metal now. But that's all that's changed.

For Poppa and my daddy, Spruill's Bridge had marked the way to Creswell. But I was looking in the other direction, toward the plantation. There, on the other side of the river, began the fields of Somerset.

Everything slowed as I turned onto the entrance drive. Flat brown acreage stretched away on either side of the arrow-straight pavement. The road and the land shimmered in the windless, midday heat. Crows sat on telephone lines. A ditch, maybe fifteen feet wide, choked with weeds, ran along the roadside, pointing the way to a dark blur in the distance.

One mile, then two, then three. My odometer rolled on, and the scene stayed the same. The blur appeared to move no closer. Then, in an instant, it took shape. Trees. More than a hundred of them, one after another, in a line that seemed to go to the horizon. Massive cypresses, each as tall as a six-story building, each five feet thick or more, all as erect and precisely spaced as a row of stiff soldiers. Cypresses are everywhere in these swampy

woods, but this wall of trees, so ordered, so intimidating, with
nothing around it but open fields, was planted by men.

Beyond the trees the fields gave way to a shaded drive and
then, the estate.

I don't know what I was hoping for. The sheer might of those
cypresses, the expanse of those drained fields, the pamphlet put
out by the state all prepared me for something magnificent. The
slave lists and bills of sale I had in my hand were the stuff of
wealth and power, testaments to the might of the man who
owned this land.

But the man was long gone. And what was left was hollow.
The ditch I now followed was clearly a canal, lined with more
cypresses and running off into a jungle of brush. Beyond the
brush, out of sight, was the shore of a lake that had once filled
this canal with rushing water. Now the ditch was dry, clogged
with trees sprouting from its bottom.

At the edge of the ditch sat the main house. No, it was not the
kind of mansion I'd seen on some plantations back in Virginia.
This was plainer, more a work of function than form, built for
sense not splendor. It was wooden, three stories, "T"-shaped,
rimmed by open porches aimed to catch the breezes that once
blew off the lake before a wild wall of thickets rose up to block
the way.

I parked and walked past the silent, empty house. Behind it sat
a cluster of outbuildings—small, plain cottages rimmed by a
tangle of untrimmed pecan, apple and crape myrtle trees. Weeds

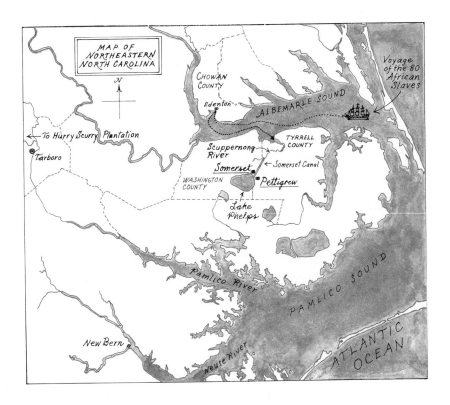

sprayed from cracks in the brick walkway that led to the largest of the outbuildings, a pale two-story house marked as the visitors' center. There wasn't a visitor in sight but me.

Beyond the center, the walkway stopped at the edge of a vast grassy field. There, on a lonely wooden sign no more than a foot high, were printed the words "Site of Slave Quarters." No buildings. No rubble. No remains. Just a sign and an open field. In one hand I held the names of almost one hundred and fifty slaves I knew belonged to the Collinses. In the other I held a pamphlet that said three hundred slaves once worked on this plantation. And this was their legacy—a single rotting sign.

I don't know why I expected anything more. I had been to colonial Williamsburg, to Jefferson's Monticello. Tourists at those places weren't shown any slave quarters. There were no monuments to the black hands that had built the white homes that the white tourists strolled through. But I was no tourist here. This was my home, my family's home. Their hands made the bricks I stood on. They dug the canal that led me here. They planted those trees that pointed the way. My people were born and were wed here. And when they died, they were buried here, somewhere.

The visitors' center was sad. Spider webs clung to the corners of the ceilings. Flies buzzed in the screenless open doors. The flies and the hum of a soft drink machine were the only sounds in the room. A woman sat behind a glass case reading a newspaper. The case was filled with books and pamphlets for other historic attractions around the state. Paintings of Josiah Collins III and his wife leaned on a dusty fireplace mantel. He looked stern, humorless. So did his wife. But then so did everyone in every nineteenth-century painting I'd ever seen.

When I asked for a tour, a teenage guide appeared and led me to what they called the "Big House." The outbuildings, I noticed, were not part of the tour. Inside one of them was the only black person in sight, a groundskeeper named Michael. He was working on one of his tools, safe from the sun. He smiled and nodded.

As the guide led me into the house, she spoke mechanically,

reciting her information as though she were leading a group of fifty. The canal, she announced, was dug by "African slaves." Inside the mansion itself, she mentioned the "hired girls" who had kept house when the Collinses lived here. Those were her only two references to the hundreds of my people who lived and worked here for almost a century.

Even the Collinses were almost forgotten in this place. Of the furniture arranged in the fourteen dark rooms, only four pieces were actually theirs. The rest were a mishmash of nineteenth-century chairs, tables, cases and chests collected to fill the empty house once it was opened as a historic site in 1967. The place was an echoing shell, the souls of the people who once lived here —black and white alike—long vanished.

99

I had arrived. Six years of searching and stumbling, and I'd finally landed here, at what felt like the emptiest, loneliest spot in the state of North Carolina. If ever I'd seen a dead end, this was it. In the most literal sense, the road I'd been following since 1977 ended here, at the swampy edge of this forgotten lake.

I was disappointed. But I felt a peace there. I felt connected to the land. I knew that a hundred and fifty years earlier my family walked over the very same land I now stood on.

I drove home that day, hit hard and hurting. But I came back to Somerset, and when I did, I found that others had walked down the path I was on, picking at the pieces of the plantation's past. I realized for the first time what an amateur I was, how little I knew about history and research compared with academic professionals and historians. I was a welfare worker, a mother. I had no college degree, no sense of the network of resources and records professional historians have at their fingertips. There wasn't a lot of material on the plantation, but what was there led me to other sources. Until then, my method had been totally trial and error, with plenty of both. I had no idea the answers to many of my questions were located on library shelves or in archives vaults. If I had known when I began what I learned from the records I found at Somerset and from professional historians I talked to over the next year, I could have found in months the answers it took me years to come to.

But there were advantages to the long road I had taken. In the censuses and courthouse books I scoured, I had collected information from what historians call primary sources. As I began reading the studies and accounts stored at Somerset and in academic libraries, I found mistakes. I knew they were mistakes because I had read firsthand the records they referred to. That gave me a confidence I hadn't had when I first began my home-grown research.

At the site, I found a copy of a Somerset plantation study written in 1954 by a state-hired expert in American history. There was also a 1971 book entitled *The Pettigrew Papers,* a thick collection of correspondence among the family who owned the plantation next to Somerset Place. When I learned a similar collection of unpublished letters among the Collinses themselves was stored at the State Archives in Raleigh, I took a week's leave and spent it there, wading through the more than two thousand letters and plantation business records that make up the "Josiah Collins Papers." Over time, I found even more: an 1839 account of Somerset Place written by a roving farm magazine editor; sketches of Josiah Collins in a 1937 book on antebellum North Carolina; the published results of a 1982 archaeological dig at Somerset; and two academic dissertations—one written in 1946 and the other in 1981—both examining life on the Pettigrew and Somerset plantations. Once their biases and inaccuracies were filtered out, these accounts told the Collins story in details I had never imagined—details I had to understand before I could piece together the story of the slaves who lived here.

It began with the lake.

Only Indians lived around this dense swamp of cypress and white cedar before the late eighteenth century. They were Roanoke Indians, the same tribe encountered by Walter Raleigh and his Lost Colony out on the coast. The Indians called this dense swamp "the haunt of beasts," but to white men, the two-hundred-thousand-acre bog was "The Little Dismal," a small cousin of its northern neighbor. And like the larger swamp, this one too had a lake at its center, which was discovered August 23, 1755.

That morning, several white hunters chased a deer deep into the mucky forest, deeper than anyone but Indians had ever gone. When the group finally decided to turn back, one of them —a man named Tarkinton—climbed a tree to see where they

Cypresses line the drive to Somerset Place. "Six years of searching and stumbling, and I'd finally landed here, at what felt like the emptiest, loneliest spot in the state of North Carolina"—Dorothy's first impression of Somerset Place.

were. Less than three hundred feet in front of him lay the sparkling blue surface of an eight-mile-wide freshwater lake. This was an age of settlers and discovery, and when Tarkinton shouted to his friends what he saw, one of them, a man named Joseph Phelps, wasted no time thrashing his way through the thickets and leaping in the water to stake his claim.

"Thus," wrote Edmund Ruffin, the magazine editor who reported on the Somerset estate in 1839, "was the name of Phelps attached to the lake, as contrary to justice, as to euphony and good taste."

It wasn't until after the American Revolution that a group of Edenton businessmen formed a company with plans to drain Lake Phelps—which was no more than six feet deep—and farm

The "Big House" at Somerset Place.

its rich bottom soil. The lake, after all, was eighteen feet higher than the Scuppernong River six miles away. A canal connecting the two could easily empty the seventeen-hundred-acre pond. At least that's what the company had in mind when it bought up more than a hundred thousand acres of land, including the lake. But after surveying the swamp between the lake and the river, the group shifted its plans. They decided that by controlled flooding, they could better use the water from the lake to turn the swampland into rice paddies. By 1784 the Lake Company had permission from the general assembly to start draining.

The company was three men: a doctor named Samuel Dickinson, whose wife was among the hostesses of the Edenton tea party; a businessman named Nathaniel Allen, whose son later became governor of Ohio and whose grandson became a U.S. senator; and Josiah Collins I, the man who would end up controlling the company and the swamp.

They called him "Captain" Collins, for the small fleet of ships he operated out of his Edenton headquarters. He was a widower with three children when he left his home in Somersetshire, England, for Boston in 1773. By the end of the war, he was in North Carolina, a place where a man with a feel for new land and cheap labor could make himself a fortune. By the time he joined Allen and Dickinson to form the Lake Company, Collins had his fortune. His ships were sailing to the Mediterranean and the Orient. He owned one of the young nation's largest rope-making businesses—later, Collins rope formed the rigging for most of the U.S. Navy's ships in the War of 1812. He lived in one of Edenton's finest waterfront homes. And he owned sixty thousand acres of undeveloped swampland across the sound.

It was that land that Collins had his eye on when he joined with Allen and Dickinson. Collins was fascinated with canals. He had seen the success of England's first canal-building boom in the 1760s. And he saw the chance to make it work here. The South was crowded with wealthy investors by the end of the war, good land was becoming scarce and speculators were already heading west to open new territory. But a few men like Collins were looking instead to develop the land still left in their own backyards, unimproved land like the swamps across the sound. George Washington had the same idea when he went into Vir-

ginia's Great Dismal. In fact, Washington and Collins suppos-
edly exchanged letters on the art of canal-building. According to
Collins family lore, Washington was so impressed with Collins
that he considered the Edenton merchant for Secretary of the
Treasury when Washington was elected President of the United
States in 1789. Collins turned the offer down, and the secretary-
ship went to Alexander Hamilton. Or so the family story goes.

When Collins joined Allen and Dickinson to form the Lake
Company late in 1784, he knew where the canal had to be built
and how. He knew he wanted to grow rice, and African—not
West Indian—slaves had that skill. And he knew he had to move
fast, because there was already talk of banning imported slaves
in North Carolina.

In 1784 Collins sent an eight-ton brig named the *Camden* to
Boston, where it was fitted out for a transatlantic voyage. The
next record of the ship is a page in the Edenton port records
showing the *Camden* arriving in Edenton Bay June 10, 1786,
from "Affirica," carrying eighty "Negroes," who cost two thousand eight hundred and forty-four pounds, plus a duty fee of
fifty-six pounds. These were the men "between 20 and 25 years
of age . . . extremely black, with elegant white teeth . . ." that
the Edenton Chamber of Commerce history said arrived on "the
brig *Guineaman.*" A "guineaman" was actually a generic term
referring to a ship that carried slaves. And the eyewitness account of "a hundred Negroes" was an inaccurate guess, according to the port records I studied.

It was the *Camden* that carried the caged men who would help dig Collins' canal.

The digging took two years. Two years of malaria-ridden mosquitoes and blood-gorged black flies feasting on the slaves' flesh. Two years of hacking through a primordial jungle, through trees and roots thick beyond comprehension. One ten-foot-thick, eight-hundred-year-old tree would be pulled aside only to reveal its roots wrapped around an even thicker tree more than a thousand years old. Collins almost never came near the site. Dickinson came once a month to care for sick or injured slaves. The day-to-day excavation was left to an overseer named Thomas Trotter, a Scottish engineer who had made his name landscaping gardens in Edenton. But this was no garden. And Trotter took no chances with his labor. He built cages around slaves as they dug, forcing them to pass the dirt and mud out through the bars.

It took two years, and many of them died, some of sickness, some of sheer exhaustion. Slaves who were not able to leave the work site at the end of a day "would be left by the bank of the canal, and the next morning the returning gang would find them dead." Those were Trotter's words.

There was no way to tell how many slaves died digging that swamp. No one kept count. All that counted was the canal, and when it was done, it was beautiful. Six miles long. Twenty feet wide. Four to fifteen feet deep. By 1790, quarters for a hundred slaves had been built, and barges were floating from the river to the lake and carrying away the timber being cut at the Lake Company sawmill, a mill powered by the steady flow of canal water. Collins' fleet of ships was soon filled with cypress planks headed for other cities and to the wood-starved Caribbean. Business was good, so good that the canal bottom was continually clogged with sawdust, and slaves were regularly sent in to shovel it out.

As the trees came down, Trotter set about designing a dike and irrigation system. The company owned one hundred and thirteen slaves in Tyrrell County in 1790, according to census records, and those slaves spent most of the next decade digging hundreds of miles of ditches, raising farmland from that swamp. Rice, hemp, and—when enough land was drained—corn were planted. Too many slaves died of disease planting rice—corn was more cost-efficient. By 1803, when the slave inventory I found in Edenton was filed, the company had begun breaking up. By 1816 Collins had bought out his partners and was in complete control of what had become a lakeside kingdom of corn and wheat. A year later he named the plantation Somerset Place, after his home in England. Although he still lived in Edenton, Collins was proud to take visitors out to his farm. Journals and magazines of the time are sprinkled with descriptions of Somerset like this one, written in 1820 by a man named Willie Mangum:

> . . . here is the finest estate in North Carolina. Sixty three thousand Acres of land in one body as rich as the banks of the Nile.

Collins had been dead a year when those words were written. In his will, he left his Edenton businesses and "the land on Lake Phelps . . . Also all the negroes, 'upwards of one hundred in number . . .'" to his son Josiah II, with the stipulation that Josiah III, who was then eleven, would inherit the plantation when he came of age.

Josiah II was fifty-six when his father died. Like his father, he never lived at Somerset. He spent his time at the family's Edenton estate instead. But he built a two-story house at the plantation for overnight business. It was called the Colony House then. More than a century later, it became the park's visitors' center—the dusty building with the soft drink machine.

Long before Josiah II took over Somerset, an Episcopal minister named Charles Pettigrew had established a smaller farm on the east side of the canal—a plantation called Bonarva—and passed it on to his son, Ebenezer. The Pettigrews never saw much of the elder Collins, who rarely visited the lake. But Josiah II was spending more time here, and according to some of the Pettigrew letters, neither Ebenezer nor his wife thought much of their new neighbors.

"They are indeed very dressy," sniffed Mrs. Pettigrew in an 1824 letter. A year later she tried hard to say something nice about Mrs. Collins. The best she could come up with was: "She bids fair to be a monstrous large woman."

Collins spent the better part of 1828 getting Somerset ready for his son to take over. In a letter written that year, Ebenezer

Pettigrew described his apprehensions about the impending arrival:

> Mr. Collins has been on the Lake the greater part of this year without his family . . . He seems to enjoy the loneliness of this place—such is the effect of age, he is very unlike his family—they are gay and fond of the world. I suppose next year his son will take possession, they have increased the number of slaves and houses and find their overseers so faithless that they must give their personal attention, the only alternative for farmers. The education of the son will cause him to pass many a wretched hour, it will be very unlike New York, the opera and amusements of various kinds which that great city affords.

When Josiah III arrived at Somerset in January 1830, the lives of everyone there—from the slaves to neighbors like the Pettigrews—were changed. The young Josiah had studied at Harvard, read law in Connecticut, married a young society woman from New Jersey and now, at twenty-two, was taking control of one of the largest farms in eastern North Carolina. He would be the first of his family to actually live at Somerset, and he wasn't about to move into any two-story hut. No, as soon as he arrived, work began on a mansion.

The Pettigrews had their doubts about the newcomers. Ebenezer Pettigrew, the son of a strait-laced minister, was uncomfortable with Collins' fast-lane background:

> . . . the young gentleman's habits of society, and his associates being of the first circle in the nation, forbid that I could be company for him long at a time or very often.

When Mrs. Pettigrew died late that year, the Collinses were

kind to Ebenezer. "They received me with a countenance which bespoke that they could weep with the weeping," he wrote. Even though he thought Collins was a poor landowner and criticized the "diletante farmer" for losing wheat crops in 1835 and 1836 to late frosts and wet weather, Pettigrew became Collins' partner in a short-lived silkworm venture. They bought forty thousand mulberry trees and planted them by the sound in an area called Pea Ridge—today it's Skinnersville. Three years after they planted the trees, the partners sold the business and Pettigrew again began writing nasty letters, as did his son, William, who had his own reason for disliking the Collins family: William Pettigrew asked Collins' sister Elizabeth Alethia to marry him in 1845, and she turned him down. The next Christmas was the first since the Collinses arrived that the Pettigrews did not spend the holiday suffering under what Ebenezer called his neighbors' "aggressive type of hospitality." William was especially happy:

> I feel relieved of a burden now that I do not dine on Christmas Day, or the day after, or at all, at my . . . neighbors. On such occasions all was ceremony and restraint; which was irksome to me, a plain, unpretending individual, who cannot easily adapt myself to the frivolity of fashionable people.

Christmas was the peak of the Collinses' entertaining season, which lasted throughout the winter and well into spring. They were known for hosting quadrilles night after night and for dinner parties that lasted until dawn. By summer, the overwhelming heat drove them out of the swamp, to their Edenton mansion, to hot springs and spas in Virginia, to family and

Josiah Collins III and his wife, Mary Riggs. Collins was the grandson of Josiah Collins I, the first owner of Somerset Place.

friends in New York. But each autumn they returned to Somerset, trying in their own way to bring culture to the swamps.

They liked to read, especially aloud, and Monday nights they gathered neighbors and whatever guests were staying in the house—the Collinses always had house guests—for a reading club, led by Josiah. Collins considered himself an excellent reader, and he especially enjoyed reading the Bible aloud to the slaves during Sunday church services in the chapel he built for them.

His slaves had no choice but to listen to Collins' voice. His white neighbors, however, were not always a willing audience. In one letter describing his stay at the Collins' house, one of Ebenezer Pettigrew's sons wrote that he was "bored to death by Mr. Collins's long winded harangues." Ebenezer himself wasted no words describing his disdain for Collins' "pretensions": "So much Pride, so much selfishness, so much vanity, so much opinionatedness, in a word so much of everything that is unami-cable." Ebenezer had a right to be a bit testy—he'd just come out on the short end of a corn deal with Collins.

Josiah Collins did like the sound of his own voice, and in 1845 he decided he particularly liked the sound of it in French. That was the year he adopted French as the household language. He hired a French tutor named Mr. Ernest, who lived in the Colony House, where he gave daily lessons to Collins' sons.

According to the Pettigrews, the Collinses' never-ending stream of house guests snickered at the family's "ludicrous" hospitality and at Josiah Collins' "domineering" personality. Everything he did, he did to excess, according to his neighbors.

When Josiah IV, the oldest son, was married in 1859, and his parents prepared him for his honeymoon, one of the Pettigrew women wrote, "I don't think ever before was known such a ridiculous amount of luggage for two persons." The Pettigrews also sneered at the wedding cake the Collinses ordered express from New York—"a sort of primogeniture looking cake."

Yet while the Pettigrews steamed, there were people who were impressed with the Collinses. One was a Dr. Edward Warren, whose father was the Collins family physician for fifty years. Warren shared his memories of Somerset Place and of Josiah II's family in an 1885 book entitled *A Doctor's Experiences in Three Continents.* First he fell over himself describing Josiah III's younger brother Hugh:

> Hugh W. Collins, the second son, stood six feet and two inches in his stockings, and though of herculean proportions his figure was

symmetrical and his carriage remarkably graceful. He had besides an exceedingly handsome and attractive face, with the regular features, soft blue eyes, and a smile of peculiar fascination, while his head was a faultless development, covered with a profusion of sunny curls, and sat on his shoulders like that of an Apollo. Though he was as lavish with his means as a prince, as gentle in nature as a girl, and as gay of spirit as a bird, he was brave to rashness, and as chivalrous as any Plumed Knight. He excelled in everything. He was the strongest man, the best horseman, the deadliest shot, the finest boxer, the fleetest skater, the greatest beau, and the most eloquent speaker in his section.

Not to mention quite a drinker, judging from Hugh's bar bills included in the Collins Collection. When Dr. Warren finally got around to the fate of poor Hugh, there wasn't much to say:

He died in 1854 in the old mansion at Edenton, of dropsy resulting from cirrhosis of the liver.

There was a little more sting in the doctor's words when he got around to Josiah III:

He esteemed *his* blood the bluest, *his* opinions the wisest, *his* tastes the truest, and everything identified with *him* the most perfect that the world contained. He was an autocrat with a will as imperious and a sway as absolute as the Czar himself; but, though impatient and arbitrary when antagonized, he was the soul of courtesy, amiability and kindness when unopposed.

And, wrote the awed doctor, the young Collins could lay out a spread:

I scarcely ever visited the "lake" without finding a large company assembled there, having as good a time as it was possible to conceive of. Such a host of servants, horses, carriages, games, boats, guns, accoutrements, musical instruments, and appliances generally for interesting and entertaining people, I never saw collected together. His table was a most sumptuous one. It groaned in fact beneath the load of every delicacy that taste could suggest, and such triumphs of the culinary art as were only possible to the well-trained darkey cooks with which his kitchen was crowded, while wines of the most ancient vintage and liquors of the choicest brand flowed around it like water from some inexhaustible spring.

When Dr. Edwards wrapped up his portrait of Josiah III, he had mixed feelings:

> He had his faults, for he was of a proud nature, and a domineering spirit, oversatisfied with himself and impatient in the face of opposition; but his virtues far outweighed his failings, and a braver, nobler and more magnificent type of humanity has seldom walked among men in any land or time.

His will and his wealth usually gave Collins his way. But nothing could help him avoid the worst tragedy of his three decades at Somerset—the drowning deaths of two of his six sons, eight-year-old Edward and ten-year-old Hugh Daves Collins. The incident was described in a letter written by William Pettigrew:

> Edward and Hugh Collins were drowned in their Father's canal on Thursday 4 P.M. Feb. 2d, 1843. They were seen by my father's servant Jim as he carried the mail over, together with two Negro boys nearly of the same age in a boat in the canal . . . midway between the dwelling house and the mill. As Jim crossed the bridge on his return, he perceived the heads of the boys above the water. He immediately gave the alarm. Mr. Collins and Joseph Newberry (the overseer) were in the field a mile or half a mile from the spot. William Newberry (under overseer) was at the mill; he immediately had the mill gates shut in order to prevent the bodies passing through them: there not being sufficient force to close the

Lake gates, they remained open until force came from the field. As soon as Jim had given the alarm, Mr. Fitzgerald (the minister at Somerset Place) and he ran to the spot. Mr. F. insisted on Jim leaping in to extricate them, but the latter refused on the ground that he would be numbed, whereupon Mr. F. leaped in himself, without any alteration in his clothing; in a short while he became numbed and had it not been for Jim's timely assistance would have sunk to rise no more, the water being ten feet deep.

In about an hour after they were first discovered, Mr. Collins and Joseph Newberry arrived together with a number of Negroes. The upper gates were closed and the lower ones opened; the water soon fell, leaving it waist deep. Joseph Newberry and Dick Blount (a Negro man) took out the children. They had been drowned a half hour or hour when they were taken from the canal.

Edward and Hugh were carried to their Father's house, and placed in separate rooms, that both might derive the utmost benefit from the fire. They were rubbed incessantly . . . but all in vain . . . My brother Charles, with others, was rubbing Hugh. After an hour or two had elapsed and their efforts were evidently unavailing, Mrs. Collins being in the same room, asked the Dr. if there was any hope—"None, madam" was the reply. Then followed a sublime scene: She kissed her child with a mother's fondness. With firmness bordering on heroism, the silent tear trickling down her cheek, she addressed him as follows—"Farewell my dear son; you are promising buds (hesitating a moment) destined to bloom in heaven, which has been my aim—my chief aim." Then taking her remaining children that were in the room to the lifeless body —said—"Come, look at your dear brother—there are but five of us now." She then took leave of the gentlemen in the room, and thanked them for their kindness.

The bodies were shrouded late in the afternoon, after tea the coffin was carried into the room, and the bodies placed in it. About 9 the family made their appearance to take farewell of the objects of their affection before the lid was closed.

On Saturday morning, soon after daylight, the coffin, containing the two brothers, was placed in my Father's barouche, bound securely with cords. Two of the gentlest horses on Mr. Collins' plantation were to draw them, a servant was to ride one of the horses, William Newberry and myself to ride in front on horse back, two Negro outriders in the rear, and Mr. Riggs (Mrs. Collins' brother) in a sulky behind the entire company. In this manner we proceeded . . . until we reached the Ferry (Macky's). Mr. and Mrs. Collins together with the gentlemen of the household, arrived at 3 o'clock, an hour later. Immediately upon their arrival the steamboat left for Edenton with its charge.

Pettigrew didn't bother mentioning what became of the slave boys whose bodies were pulled up with the Collinses. He didn't even mention their names.

116

With so much water around—the canal ran past the mansion's front door, and the lake was just down the lawn—the other Collins children had several near misses with drowning. One son, George, fell from a bridge into the mud of an irrigation ditch, where he was stuck for hours. It was dark when his apparently lifeless body was finally found and pulled out. He survived, and a year later gave his parents another sleepless night when he and two slaves, while returning from a bear hunt, capsized their boat on the lake and were presumed dead until a search party found them the next morning.

Another son, William Kent Collins, died another way. Racing his horse along the canal toward the house, he was thrown against an elm and was killed instantly. They say Josiah Collins was so anguished that he fastened a heavy chain around the tree, which over the next few years cut into its trunk and strangled it to death.

For all his problems at home, Collins remained a successful farmer. Once he stopped experimenting with wheat and concentrated on corn, his business flourished. It was said that when Commodore Matthew Perry opened Western trade with Japan in 1853, he carried samples of Collins corn with him. Family lore again, but there is no doubt Collins owned one of the largest farms in North Carolina in 1860. Somerset consisted of more than four thousand acres that year, and, according to census records, three hundred and twenty-eight slaves worked those fields. That made Collins the third-largest slaveholder in the state. If the one hundred and seventy-seven slaves he owned at his four smaller properties—two in Edenton and two in the central part of the state—were included, Collins was the second-largest slaveholder in North Carolina.

But it wasn't just his slaves that made Collins a wealthy man. He also knew how to make a dollar off the poor whites in the area. He charged them top prices to mill their corn with his machines, and he rarely missed the local sheriff's sales, where poor white farmers' property was auctioned off for unpaid debts. At one such sale, a farmer who was late on a seven-dollar bill saw Collins buy all his household furnishings and livestock— seven hogs, four cattle, a bed, a chest, two tables, some crockery and a cupboard—for seventy-five dollars.

By 1860, however, Collins' lavish lifestyle was threatened. The shadow of civil war was spreading across Somerset and the South. Abolition had become a hot topic in living rooms throughout Carolina, and of course Collins was on fire with the subject, blasting the abolitionists at every opportunity, and driving even more guests away in the process.

"Our excellent neighbors," wrote one of the Pettigrews in 1860, "appear to me as rabid on one side of the subject as the Abolitionists are on the other."

"Their way of hitting at the North all the time," she commented in another letter, "and allowing nothing said contra, is . . . neither good manners, nor good sense. . . ."

By 1860 Collins was plagued with migraine headaches that made him more moody and erratic than ever. His wife had a stroke that same year. When war began the next year, both Collins and the Pettigrews paid to outfit local companies of Confederate soldiers. Mrs. Collins even sewed long underwear for the troops. In 1862, Josiah IV and Arthur—two of the three surviving Collins boys—enlisted with an Edenton company. Later, George joined the staff of General James Johnson Pettigrew—one of Ebenezer's seven sons.

By the time his boys were suiting up to fight, Josiah Collins had packed his bags and moved. By April 1862, when Federal troops captured the Carolina coast, Collins had moved his wife to a smaller family plantation in Hillsborough, west of Durham, one hundred and sixty miles inland from Somerset. That summer a Federal gunboat sailed down the Scuppernong, up the Somerset Canal and docked at Collins' mill. The twelve Union soldiers aboard took bushels of corn and wheat, but according to the plantation's minister, Reverend George Patterson, who described the visit in a letter sent to Collins at Hillsborough, the Yankees left the slaves alone:

I'm happy to say that all of our servants behaved with great prior-
ity. None were carried away by the yankees and not one of them so
far as I can learn was at all desirous to run away.

Patterson did mention later in the same letter that one of the
soldiers raped a slave named Lovey in the cook house, but other
than that, he wrote, everything went well.

Six days later, however, the Yankees came back, and this time
there was trouble. Thirty soldiers arrived, demanding horses
and talking with the slaves about freedom and working for
wages. When Patterson ordered one of the slaves to guard an
orchard near the house, the slave disobeyed and instead went to
help the soldiers bridle the animals they were taking. That slave,
described by Patterson as "extremely wicked" and "worthy of
punishment," was Fred Littlejohn, my great-grandpa Alfred's
father.

When Collins got word of the Yankees' second visit, he pan-
icked. He immediately wrote his overseers at Somerset to select
the slaves needed to keep that plantation operating. The rest,
except for the elderly unable to walk, were to be marched inland,
out of the Yankees' reach. On the night of October 14, two
hundred and twenty-seven Somerset slaves—including Fred Littlejohn and his family—were led by armed guards out of the
swamp to a Collins plantation called Hurry Scurry in Franklin
County, one hundred and twenty miles away.

Neither of the Collinses' two "up country" plantations were as
large as Somerset. When the slaves arrived, Collins had no work

for them, so he hired them out to a nearby railroad company, to Confederate Army hospitals and to other farmers in the area. Meanwhile, sixty-five slaves were left behind at Somerset, some of whom began sleeping in the woods at night, hoping the Yankees would arrive before they too were marched away from freedom. Some planters in the area surrounded their field workers with armed guards during the day. Collins was apparently too busy controlling his "up country" slaves to pass this kind of order to Somerset.

At the news that Yankees were in the Albemarle, the Pettigrew slaves "stampeded," and William Pettigrew had to call in troops to surround his slave houses. He, too, marched almost all his slaves to Chatham County, south of Hillsborough. The ones that remained became "indolent and out of control." Local "Buffaloes"—renegade troops under no one's command—plundered both estates. Local poor whites joined in, taking particular pleasure in ransacking the Collins mansion. One pillager went so far as to steal Collins' entire library—from books to furniture—and reconstruct it in his own living room.

By the spring of 1863, Lincoln had delivered his Emancipation Proclamation, and Federal troops had ridden out to Somerset to tell the slaves they were free. Most of them stayed on the plantation, unsure of their new status. They began working more for themselves and less for the overseer. Josiah Collins died in June of that year, but his overseer at Somerset kept the plantation sputtering until Mrs. Collins and her sons returned at the end of the war.

In 1865, Mary Collins and two of her sons came back to revive Somerset. But they couldn't do it. Most of the slaves from Hurry Scurry and Hillsborough had returned to Somerset, to familiar ground and family. George Collins refused to pay them wages, and they refused to work for the scanty shares of crops he offered them. Most of them soon moved off the plantation— house servants went to Edenton to find work, and field hands settled on land around the estate. And some moved even farther —to Virginia and points north. By 1866 only two former slaves were left at Somerset. That left Mrs. Collins to do her own housework. Her sons cut firewood and took care of other chores they had always left to the slaves. The best they could find in the way of hired help were three local white women.

The last dinner party held in the Collins mansion took place in the spring of 1866, and it was a pathetic affair. Nine guests, including Charles Pettigrew, were there. Mrs. Collins was close to losing her plantation at auction, but this night she spared no expense, covering the table with ham, lamb, turkey and even lobster. Still, things had changed since the days of slave waiters and cooks. The white women who prepared and served this dinner sat down to share it with the guests, a "novel procedure" noticed by Pettigrew. The meal itself, he noted, "was a very quiet one," hosted by Josiah IV, a different man from his father.

"He is very quiet," wrote Pettigrew, "and only now and then makes any attempt at fun. He is not able to take his father's place. What a change!"

What a change. In 1870, to cover a ten-thousand-dollar debt

left by her husband, Mrs. Collins signed away the four thousand four hundred and twenty-eight acres that was Somerset Place. She continued to live in the mansion until her death two years later. Josiah IV died in 1890, and by 1902, Josiah V had moved to Seattle, according to a sketch written that year by George Collins.

After it was first signed away, Somerset went into a sixty-year free fall, tumbling from the hands of one owner to another's, eventually slipping into control of a nearby bank in the 1920s. In 1937 the property was bought by the federal government and became one of the New Deal's resettlement projects. Poor whites were brought down from the mountains and given sixty-acre pieces of the plantation to farm. Around the outer edges of the estate, black tenant farmers and sharecroppers—many of them former Somerset slaves—scraped a living from the land they had moved onto when they were set free.

In 1939, both the Pettigrew and Somerset estates were bought by the state and turned into Pettigrew State Park, named after General James Johnson Pettigrew—George Collins' Civil War commander—who was shot at the Battle of Gettysburg and died soon after. The Pettigrew home was in ruins, so it was the mansion and surrounding buildings of Somerset Place that were protected, restored in the early 1950s and opened as a historic site in 1967.

So that was the Collins story. Not quite as succinct or clean as the brochure account. Not terribly different from so many stories of the rise and fall of Southern aristocrats. I understood the Collinses now—their pride and their pretensions. I could stand there, at the edge of that swamp, and I could almost hear the music and the laughter drifting out of the "Big House" as the sun set across the fields. I wondered what it had sounded like to the slaves who would have stood in this spot, looking up at the glow of those windows as the night sounds of the swamp rose behind their own lakeside cabins.

They were the people on whose backs the Collins fortune was built. When they were set free, that family was ruined. As simple as that. I could now see Somerset through the eyes of the Collinses. I could stand in the living room and watch their guests step through the front door. I could ride with Collins through his fields, counting acreage and bushels of corn. But I had yet to climb off the horse and see how those fields looked to the people who tilled them. I had yet to step into the kitchen with the cooks who prepared the food. I had no idea where the slaves went when the Collinses went to bed. And I still needed to know who, among the generations of black people who walked this lakeshore, were my relatives.

Among the books and papers before me, the white side of the Somerset story was easy to read.

The black side took more time.

123

VOICES FROM THE PAST

They are dead now, all of them. The Collinses, the Pettigrews and their slaves. Nineteenth-century ghosts. But even now, they are still apart, white and black, as separated in death as they were when they were living.

The whites left snapshots of their lives behind. In letters and ledger books they told me who they were and how they lived. I knew what the Collinses ate, how they dressed, where they slept, how they spoke. They spoke on paper, and their voices can still be heard a century after their bodies were put in the ground. There is little that is magical about lives like that, little to imagine, little room for mystery when the mundane is so specifically preserved.

The black people whose names I held in my hand left nothing.

What they wrote, neither they nor their masters kept. And when they spoke, really spoke, it was only to one another. The voices their masters heard were not the voices they shared among themselves. When they died, their real voices went with them. And the echoes that were left became mystery, then more. The mystery became magic. It's that way with the dead—the less we know about the lives they led, the more we make them myths when they are gone. We fill the void with our own imagining, with our own hopes.

That is what I had done as I worked my way to Somerset. Because of the very fact that all I had were lists of slave names and dates culled from courthouse records and company account books, I wrapped each of those names in an aura of wonder, of richness. Once I arrived at the place where they lived, I realized there was the chance I would be robbing that richness by digging into the reality of their pasts. In a way I was intruding, peeling away their mystery by reaching for the concrete, the three-dimensional. In a way it seemed right to leave my ancestors among the mists of myth, to keep them apart from the Collinses—to allow them in death to be more than the people who owned them in life.

But that would be to deny their own very real lives, to put my dreams above theirs. I was here now, at Somerset. I had the names. I had the place. I had to go on, to piece together their existence—as individuals; as a group.

There were no straightforward, firsthand accounts of slave life

Slave cabins and the rear of the mansion at Somerset Place,
c. 1900–15.

at Somerset. Only references among the Collinses' and Pet-tigrews' correspondence. Costs of slaves in old ledger books. Entries of money paid for slave shoes and buttons.

Tiny slivers of reality, mere shavings of the past, disjunctive fragments of time.

Mention of a persistent runaway in an overseer's letter. Plantation inventories listing slaves by cabin, telling me who lived with whom, giving me a sense of families, but only a sense. An archaeologist's reconstruction describing where those cabins stood, how they were built, even their color—white.

I walked into a church where my ancestors had sung both before and after they were told they were free. There were records in that church's registry—more names, more dates of births, of marriages, of deaths. I pushed through brambles and sank in mud, hunting for family cemeteries in the woods beyond the plantation, where the emancipated slaves who moved off Somerset after the war buried their dead and where I found gravestones that gave me more names, always more names.

I studied books and historical articles on the African slave trade, on slave life on other plantations in other states, on runaway slaves in eighteenth-century North Carolina, even on naming patterns among slaves and owners in the antebellum South. I read interviews with former North Carolina slaves collected by the federal government during the 1930s, accounts that included one precious conversation with a former Somerset slave.

As these scattered splinters of the past piled before me, images took shape. Some of the pieces were linked without question. Others required logic and deduction to join them together. Sometimes I had no choice but to guess my way from one to another. The lives I resurrected were shaped by facts, but they remained ghostly—cryptic outlines shimmering with the dignity of vagueness.

The Africans were the vaguest.

All I knew of the *Camden*'s journey was that the eighty-ton brig was sent north in the winter of 1784 with a hold full of tobacco, pork, beef, rice and molasses and came back to Edenton a year and a half later carrying eighty Africans. In between—probably during the "fitting out" in Boston—I was sure the brig's hold was loaded with a healthy supply of New England rum. When

American ships shopped for African slaves in the eighteenth and nineteenth centuries, rum was the going currency. Anyone who ever took a high school history class knows about the triangular slave trade system: rum for slaves for molasses for rum. But now I was seeing it in human, not historical terms. These were my relatives being bartered for liquor. So when I read a passage like this one from a book called *Black Cargos: A History of the Atlantic Slave Trade,* the idea was more than academic:

> . . . at the home port the vessel would take on a cargo chiefly or entirely of rum. In Africa it was exchanged for as many slaves as it would buy. On the return trip slaves were sold in the West Indies and a part of its proceeds would be invested in molasses, usually in French or Spanish Islands where it was cheaper. On the final leg of the voyage, the vessel would carry the molasses back to New England to be distilled to make more rum, to buy more slaves.

129

Such efficiency. But the *Camden*'s journey was different. First, the standard slaving vessel was crammed with as many bodies as it could carry. "Tight packing," they called it, and the traders counted on losing an average of 30 percent of their slaves during the voyage—to heat, disease and, often, suicide. Three out of ten human beings were written off like so many spoiled vegetables. A hundred-ton ship typically carried two hundred and fifty slaves, most of whom were unclothed, sleeping in their own excrement and crying for help in languages their captors had no reason to understand.

The *Camden*'s load of eighty was a light one—"loose packed." And the fact that a grist mill was installed on board to grind fresh meal to feed the slaves indicates that Collins and his partners wanted healthy bodies to step off that ship. Their canal was a special project, and these men were taking care of the human machinery—the *skilled* labor they'd sought in Africa—that would dig it. There was no humanity in their kindness—it was just good business. They weren't pampering their cargo—the Lake Company account books listed "handcuffs and fetters" bought for the *Camden.*

I had no way of knowing exactly where the *Camden* loaded its slaves. I could find no records of the ship's African destination. But the history books I studied told me the western Gold Coast —where tribes such as the Ashanti, Bono, Brong and Fante had moved during the seventeenth century, and where European colonists had set up trading posts earlier than that—was the center of African slave trade when the *Camden* sailed there in 1785. If the brig did dock there, the natives it picked up would have shared a common language—Akan—and a common culture. Indeed, after talking with a professor of African studies I met through a friend from my church in Norfolk, I learned that the African-sounding names I had found among the company's 1803 inventory included anglicized versions of Akan names: "Quaminy" for the Akan "Kwame"; "Donkey" for "Donko"; "Cuff" for "Kofi."

There was another reason the *Camden* would have wanted West African slaves: Rice. The Lake Company needed bodies that could resist the malaria that festered in the swamps where the canal was to be dug and in the wet fields where the rice

would be grown. Not only were West Africans skilled rice planters who had grown the crop on the Windward Coast for centuries, but they were known to have a relative resistance to malaria,
an immunity we now know is linked to the sickle-shaped blood
cells of black people from tropical climates. But Ebenezer Pettigrew didn't know anything about sickle cells when he wrote a
letter commenting on the African slave labor. All he knew was
the necessity for ditch-diggers, a need he described in a blunt
letter:

> Negroes are a troublesome property, and unless well managed, an
> expensive one, but they are indispensable in this unhealthy and
> laborious country, for these long canals that are all important in
> rendering our swamplands valuable must be dug by them or not at
> all.

131

The canals were dug by what the Lake Company account book
called "the new negros." And even with their "immunity," they
fell sick. "Ague," "flux" and "bilious fever"—each a different
way of describing malaria—were rampant. If the sickness was
treated at all, the treatment was quinine, a poison that usually
made the patient violently ill. Survive the cure, they said, and
you'd have little problem with the disease. Samuel Dickinson
was a doctor, and according to the Lake Company's account
books, his obligations included treating the medical needs of the
slaves. Each month's ledger book entry for "medicine for Negroes" was mostly for quinine.

But worse than the Africans' hideous voyage to America or
the disease-ridden swamps they were herded into once they got

here was the emotional shock of being ripped from their tradition-soaked homeland and the unspeakable anguish of ending up in a completely unrecognizable land. According to Trotter, the company's overseer at the canal site, some of those first eighty Africans were actually driven into Lake Phelps by their grief:

> At night they would begin to sing their native songs . . . In a short while they would become so wrought up that, utterly oblivious to the danger involved, they would grasp their bundles of personal effects, swing them on their shoulders, and setting their faces towards Africa, would march down into the water singing as they marched till recalled to their senses only by the drowning of some of the party.

It wasn't long before Collins ordered the singing stopped. Losing slaves to the lake was not cost-efficient.

Still, the Africans held on to what they could of their culture. An archaeology team from Duke University studied the Somerset site in 1982 and discovered pieces of "crude" pottery. In an article entitled "Digging up Slave History," the team leader—a Duke history professor named Peter Wood—noted that simple, unglazed pottery had been found at eighteenth-century colonial sites for years and had always been assumed to be Indian. But this stoneware, he concluded, was "definitely Afro-American pottery." So, he guessed, were many of the shards that had been found at other southeast Atlantic sites and assumed to be Indian.

"Archaeologists have been excavating these fragments for

View of Somerset Place from Lake Phelps, c. 1936.

years without understanding them," wrote Wood. "They were wearing cultural blinders that prevented them from recognizing evidence that was right in front of them."

The message is obvious: Even scientists can be racists. Well intentioned, maybe. Unaware of their biases, hopefully. But racists nonetheless.

By recognizing the Somerset evidence for what it was, it was easy for Wood to give the clay fragments a simple, obvious explanation, one that escaped his colleagues at similar sites: "Perhaps they were made by men who had watched women create pottery in Africa and who were now obliged to make bowls on their own."

Men without women. This was another adjustment my African ancestors had to make. The *Camden*'s cargo was almost all men. Women and children were not needed to dig a canal. These men left behind their African families and were forced to form new ones in North Carolina—yet another adjustment, since they shared neither the language nor the culture of American-reared slaves.

The early account books I found were filled with records of Collins and his partners "hiring out" their own personal slaves to the Lake Company, sending these American-born slaves from Edenton to the Somerset site. While the Africans dug, these "company slaves" built roads and cabins. By 1790 there were three slave houses standing along the shore of the lake. By that year thirty-three of the company's Edenton-based slaves had joined the Africans in the swamp. And that was the year Guinea Jack and Fanny Collins were married.

Guinea Jack was one of the eighty Africans loaded on the *Camden.* He was the oldest of the Somerset slaves still living when Josiah Collins III took over the plantation and began keeping extensive records of his human property. Guinea Jack was eighteen when he arrived at Lake Phelps. And he was still alive fifty-three years later, when his name appeared on an 1839 Collins slave inventory next to that of his wife of forty-nine years, Fanny. I couldn't find out whether Fanny was part of that African shipment or was one of Collins' Edenton slaves. All I know is that she and her husband survived the early years and had six children, only two of whom were still living in 1839. I also know Guinea Jack clung to at least one of his African customs—at the same time he was married to Fanny, he had another wife named Grace, who bore him one son. Although the practice faded as later generations of Somerset-born slaves replaced the original Africans, polygamy was not uncommon in the plantation's early years.

I don't know how Guinea Jack lived, what his job was once the canal was finished, how he blended his African culture and language with those of the English-speaking slaves he met at Somerset. The picture of daily life on the plantation before Josiah III arrived in 1830 is a sketchy one. But just scanning the lines from the account books gave me telling glimpses into the early years. In 1787—a year after the Africans arrived and the same year the U.S. Constitution was signed—the following entries were among dozens recorded in the Lake Company logbooks:

135

> April 19—Nine pounds to Nathaniel Allen "for 3 days hire of Caesar."
>
> May 22—Three pounds "paid Caleb Benbridge for apprehending Negro Sam."
>
> May 24—One shilling to Josiah Collins "for Beef & Bread for Negroes."
>
> May 26—Two pounds, nine shillings to Samuel Dickinson "for sundry medicines for Negroes this month."
>
> May 26—Six shillings to Ebenezer Spruill "for bringing home runaway Negroe."
>
> June 11—Four pounds, six shillings "paid Wilkins for apprehending Negro Sam."
>
> June 27—Eight shillings "for 4 qts. Rum for Negroes."

July 1—Four pounds "paid Joseph Oliver for building two Negroe houses."

July 10—Twenty pounds, fourteen shillings "for 138 yds. Asnaburg for Negroes clothes."

July 10—Two pounds "pd. James Ambrose for taking up two Negroes."

August 21—Seventeen pounds, fifteen shillings "paid for making 60 shirts, 43 shifts, 60 pr. trousers & 33 coats."

December 4—Two pounds, sixteen shillings "paid John Alexander for hogs stolen by our Negroes."

December 4—Four pounds "paid John Porter for taking up Smart & Sambo."

As the canal was being dug, Collins and his partners were buying clothing, building housing, even supplying rum for their slaves' medicinal needs. All the necessities, as Collins probably saw it.

But still there were runaways.

It didn't make sense for Collins to beat or whip the slaves who ran—he needed able bodies. If slaves like Sambo (who was also called Sam) or Smart insisted on slipping into the swamp every chance they got, Collins didn't waste time with discipline. He simply sold them. An account book entry for April of 1789 listed Smart and Sam running away yet again. But this time, there was another entry in the same month, for the "net sale of sugar received for the Negro Smart, sold in the West Indies."

In the end, sugar was worth more to the company than Smart. And there was a particular, brutal sting to his punishment—it would have been one thing to sell Smart to another plantation, but to dump him in the West Indies was, for the family he left

136

behind, like sending him to the other side of the world. They could not even hope to ever see or hear of him again.

Another chronic runaway was Yellowman Dave Hortin, one of Ebenezer Pettigrew's slaves. By 1820, Hortin and another Pettigrew slave named Pompey had earned a reputation for several escape attempts. Each time they left, it took nothing more than an ad in the local newspaper and they were found and returned. So Pettigrew probably expected a quick response from the following notice, printed in a September 1820 issue of the Edenton *Gazette:*

50 DOLLARS REWARD
My negro Pomp and Dave having run away I will give the above reward to any one who will deliver them to me or half the sum for the delivery of either one.

But this time the pair stayed at large for more than a year before they were spotted several counties away by a man who threatened to "kill them on the spot." That's how the man described his warning in a letter to Pettigrew:

Their reply was we cannot drop our guns but if you will not kill us we will lower the muzzles and come to you if you will give your word you will not kill nor try to take us. I answered I would not and ordered them to come and speak to me. One yellow man said he belonged to you the other refused to answer. Keeping their guns in good order to defend themselves and would not get nearer to each other than about 10 steps. The yellow boy appeared to be short 20 years of age and said he belonged to you. I tried to prevail on him to go home he bitterly refused and said he would die first.

Both Hortin and Pompey got away that day. Pompey was not

caught until a year later. And Hortin, who Pettigrew called "a prized intelligent negro," stayed free even longer. It wasn't until 1823, more than two years after Hortin left, that the following entry was recorded on a Pettigrew expense sheet:

> Reward for catching mulatto Dave who was runaway to New Bern 24.3 months $125.00 paid fees and expense of bringing home.

A year after he was brought home, Hortin married Betty Brickhouse, one of Collins' Somerset slaves. And suddenly—not coincidentally—he became one of Pettigrew's model servants, trusted enough that Pettigrew eventually sent him unaccompanied to a nearby town to pick up a runaway himself. By the 1840s, Hortin was a slave overseer for the Pettigrews and had nine children, who lived with Betty in one of the Collins slave cabins. Hortin spent his days working for Pettigrew and his evenings with his family at Somerset, an arrangement that was common with slaves marrying between the two plantations. Today, there is a favorite hunting spot in the woods near Bonarva that folks call "Dave's Grave." No one knows exactly where it is among the bushes and briers, but it's Yellowman who is buried in that spot.

The web of a family gave Dave Hortin and other slaves like him the support and sense of community they needed to survive. And it gave their masters what they needed. Besides the promise of multiplying generations of slave offspring, all of whom would belong to the owner, marriage kept a slave at home. Collins not only allowed his slaves to have families—he encouraged them.

138

He knew a man wouldn't get far in the swamp with a woman and children in tow. And most men weren't about to leave a family behind.

But Collins did even more than just encourage his slaves to marry. The company's early records were filled with purchases of women and children who had been separated from their husbands by earlier sales. Collins was actually reuniting families at Somerset. And among the couples he brought back together were Peter and Elsy Littlejohn—the roots of my own direct family tree.

When I had first discovered Elsy's name among the thirty-two slaves listed on the 1826 bill of sale between John Littlejohn and Josiah Collins, I had no idea of the circumstances of that sale. Now I understood. Elsy was born and raised on the Edenton plantation that Littlejohn inherited from his father William. Peter was on the Collins estate next door, where he ended up after being sold twice as a boy. Slaves were free to come and go between those plantations, just as the Somerset and Bonarva slaves were allowed to mix. By 1815, when Elsy was nineteen and Peter was thirty-three, the couple had their first child and, through a marriage between the Collins and Littlejohn families, Peter had become Littlejohn property. When Collins moved Peter to Somerset, he realized Peter was torn from his family. In buying those thirty-two Littlejohn slaves in 1826, Collins was reuniting Elsy and the six children she had by then—including my great-great-grandfather Fred—with their father at Somerset.

When Josiah III arrived in 1830, there were one hundred and eighty-three slaves living at the plantation. An 1821 map found in the State Archives showed three lakefront slave quarters, each forty-by-twenty feet, two stories high, with a large fireplace for cooking and heat. I was amazed at the dimensions. These weren't the one-family cabins I had imagined from everything I'd read about slavery—they were barracks, packed with several families in each of four rooms. The 1843 list I had showed "as many as fifteen" people living in one of those cabins. On a later slave inventory I found, there were thirty names listed in one of the barracks. Collins clothed his slaves like an army—in outfits bought and sewed in bulk—and they were housed the same way. This was a labor camp.

140

By 1843, according to the detailed slave inventory taken by Josiah III, the camp was a small city. Twenty-one more cabins had been built along the lakefront, most of them one-room buildings, eighteen feet square. That year, two hundred and eighty-five slaves were listed by name, age, cabin and room on the plantation's inventory.

I could read that list and hear one-year-old Virginia Bennett crying and keeping awake the other four children and four adults in Cabin 24.

I could see twenty-six-year-old Fred Littlejohn and his wife Naomi singing their two babies to sleep in Cabin 16, which they shared with James Baum, his wife Dinah and their five children.

And I could listen to Old Suck, the seventy-one-year-old ma-

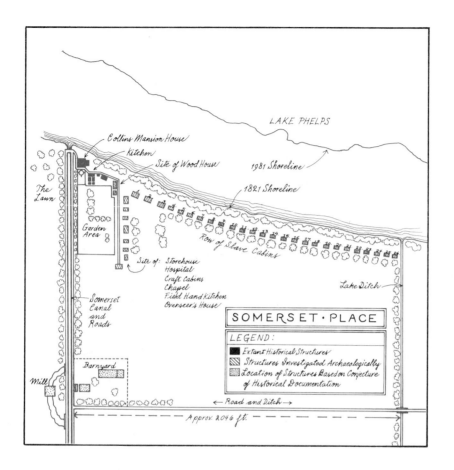

The following labels appear on the map:

LAKE PHELPS

Collins Mansion House
Kitchen
Site of Wood House
1981 Shoreline
1821 Shoreline

The Lawn

Garden Area

Row of Slave Cabins

Site of: Storehouse
Hospital
Craft Cabins
Chapel
Field Hand Kitchen
Overseer's House

Lake Ditch

Somerset Canal and Roads

SOMERSET · PLACE

LEGEND:
■ Extant Historical Structures
▨ Structures Investigated Archaeologically
▦ Location of Structures Based on Conjecture of Historical Documentation

Barnyard

Mill

← Road and Ditch →

— — — Approx. 2046 ft. — — —

triarch of her line, sitting by her upstairs window in Cabin 1, watching the moon glint off the surface of the lake and telling stories of the old days to children and grandchildren who even then assumed Somerset had been there forever.

Old Suck. She was fourteen when she was bought by Josiah Collins in Edenton the same year the Africans were unloaded at Somerset. The next year she was sent out to the site, where she stayed the rest of her life. Her first child, born when she was twenty-three, was named Trotter, probably fathered by one of the overseer's slaves. Her next was Ben, most likely named for Ben the brickmason. Suck had several mates—I had no way of telling exactly how many. But she was careful in her choice of each of them, marrying only those slaves in a prestigious position, setting a trend that her own eight children and their children after them carried on—throughout the eighty-year life of Somerset's slave community there were more artisans and house servants in Suck's family line than in any other at Somerset.

By the time Suck was a great-grandmother heading a household of twenty-four in Cabin 1, a pecking order among the slaves —from the lowly field hands to the elite house servants—had been established by Josiah III. Established with a purpose. This was just another means of control, and from his first days on the plantation, Collins felt he needed all the control he could get. He had been at Somerset only one year—hardly time enough to build his fourteen-room mansion—when he heard the news that became every slaveowner's nightmare. A thirty-one-year-old southeastern Virginia slave named Nat Turner had had a vision:

> I saw white spirits and black spirits engaged in battle and the sun was darkened, the thunder rolled in the heavens, and blood flowed in the streams . . . the time was fast approaching when the first should be last and the last should be first.

That time arrived the night of August 22, 1831. Over the next two days, fifty-five white men, women and children were axed or stabbed to death by Turner and his rebels. The slaves who followed him were immediately captured or killed, but Turner himself, hiding in the countryside around Dismal Swamp, sleeping in caves, remained at large for two months. When he was finally caught, he shared his articulate confessions with his defense lawyer. Then, on November 11, Nat Turner was hanged.

But slaveowners throughout the South continued to shake with fear. Turner's rebellion occurred less than a hundred miles from Somerset. Collins was alarmed that the spirit would spread. Indeed, his neighbor Ebenezer Pettigrew struggled for several years thereafter with a "crime wave" among his slaves. There were a rash of break-ins and stealing at Bonarva. During Christmas of 1835, while Pettigrew was away on business, his overseer reported "a big frolic," during which "the Pettigrew Negroes entertained slaves from neighboring plantations, had a feast, used the master's horse to gallivant Negro girls around the country side, and, in general misbehaved."

Collins moved quickly to keep his slaves under control. As his mansion was finished and new slave cabins were built, he drew clear lines between owner and property. His upstairs master bedroom looked out across a road to the slave quarters, which were surrounded with a fence. The road, the fence—the lines were unmistakably marked. No longer was there a flow on the grounds, a free mingling of blacks and whites. No longer was there an absentee owner and a loose affiliation with outnumbered overseers. Now there was a master in residence, with a house that needed staffing. Now there was a necessity for dis-

143

tinctions. Only house servants were allowed near the Collins mansion. Field slaves were not even to approach the master's family, much less talk to them. Uriah Bennett was eighty-three when he was approached in 1937 by a federal government interviewer who asked him to share his memories of boyhood as a Somerset slave. His testimony included a succinct description of Collins' caste system:

> The field hands were separate from those in the house. No other slaves were allowed to go to the house. If you wanted to see the master, you had to see the servant, and the servant told the master.

144

Layers upon layers. Not only was any sense of community between blacks and whites obliterated, but Collins was subtly setting the slaves against themselves. Suddenly, there were classes even among the oppressed. The field hands—who worked farthest from the mansion, who handled the dirtiest, lowliest tasks, and who were the darkest skinned—were held in the least esteem. The artisans and skilled craftsmen—who worked on the mansion's grounds and were actually paid small wages for special projects—were more respected and rewarded. And the cooks and servants—who actually worked in the master's household—were the cream of Collins' crop. The household staff were by far the best clothed and most well fed, showpieces of Collins' wealth, just as well kept as his china and carpets. They were also the fairest-skinned blacks on the plantation, white-jacketed mulattoes with a not-so-subtle message

Somerset Place mansion fronted by Lake Phelps, c. 1900–15.

from the master: The whiter you are, the better—even if you're black.

Of course that put the yellow-skinned house servants in a no-win position on the plantation. To the whites, they were still slaves, still black. And to the blacks, they were half-breeds, diluted, no longer of the race. And, of course, they were resented for the privileges they enjoyed.

But no black at Somerset was more alone than Charlotte Cabarrus, the Collins family's personal nursemaid. Not only was Charlotte fair-skinned, but she was free—the only free black at Somerset. Her ancestor Rose had been emancipated in 1735 by her owner, Augustus Cabarrus, brother of Stephen Cabarrus, one of Edenton's most prominent politicians. When Stephen died in 1807, his will set several of his own seventy-three slaves free—some of whom were Rose's offspring. Among them was Charlotte.

By 1830, Josiah Collins III hired Charlotte, and he brought her with him when he set up house at Somerset that year. It was convenient for Collins to have a free black in the household—he wasn't allowed to bring slaves with him to the family's Long Island home, since slaves were outlawed in New York. In Charlotte, he had a portable nursemaid he could take with him when he went north, although it's questionable how "free" she really was. According to account book entries, Charlotte was paid one hundred dollars a year for her services—hardly compensation for being a complete outcast. She was the highest-ranking of Somerset's house slaves, the only actual "servant," the only one who was paid, and the only one who actually lived in the mansion, in her own third-floor bedroom. She was closer to Collins than any of the slaves, and that meant they kept their distance from her. The slaves, even the lowliest field hands, at least had one another. Charlotte had no one. When she died in that third-floor bedroom during the Civil War, it was as an odd prisoner of an unshared freedom.

Sometimes Collins seemed to have conquered by dividing, by setting his slaves apart—from him, and from one another. There was nothing terribly imaginative about this man. Nothing innovative. He was no great thinker, no creative genius. He simply

146

took his circumstances and with precise calculation, squeezed every dollar he could out of every acre he planted and every slave he owned. The best and the worst that could be said about Josiah Collins III—and about so many men like him, not only then but today—is he was a good businessman.

And he was. By the late 1830s, there was a carefully orchestrated rhythm to slave life at Somerset, a rhythm that was uninterrupted until the Civil War. Somerset was a farm, and life there was geared to the seasons. Except for a one-day vacation at Thanksgiving and a week at Christmas, the slaves worked each weekday from sunup to sundown and Saturdays from sunup until noon. While the cooks and house servants took care of the Collinses' needs, the artisans and laborers kept the mill, canals and fields in operation.

And the hands worked the farm.

January was a month for clearing logs and buried trees from the frozen fields, readying the dirt for plowing. Women hauled the cut wood away. Even in fields that had been cleared for years, underground logs were routinely pushed to the surface by the freezing and thawing of the earth, emerging like slumbering giants. They were huge, moving them was a mammoth task and injuries were common. One record of a visiting doctor describes him tending a Somerset slave who had been smashed by a swinging log. The "comminuted fracture of the left Scapule"—a broken shoulder—was treated with bandages and six weeks' rest, after which the man returned to work "without any deformity apparent." A woman slave named Becky Brutus was not so lucky. By 1848, when she was twenty, Becky had "lost both legs by amputation," after they were crushed by a falling log.

January was also a time to clear drainage ditches of growth and debris, so the young corn wouldn't drown when the first spring rains arrived. Women and children took this job, and they also handled the weeds, which grew eight feet high in fallow fields and had to be cut to make way for the spring planting.

The plowing began in late January and continued through March. By 1850 there were seventeen plows on the plantation, and all of them were in the fields by March. While the men plowed, women and children went through the fields pulling old cornstalks, clearing the way for the hoeing that would come later.

148

In April the planting began. By 1839, Collins had fourteen hundred acres in corn each season, rotating unused fields to keep the soil rich. When weeds began sprouting in May, it took every field hand to keep the knee-high corn from being choked to death by creeping partridge peas and chickweed. May was also the time for women to begin raking out the deeper ditches and canals.

By June the corn had grown high enough that weeds were hardly a problem. That left the field hands free to harvest the wheat, which had been planted the previous autumn. His father had given up growing wheat commercially, but Josiah III still raised enough to make bread for his home and for his slaves.

Through June and July the slaves harvested and stored the

wheat. August and September were maintenance months, when the slaves cleared more canals and ditches, broke clods in the fields, hauled straw and cut hay. In September and October, women leveled and shored up the canal bank roads, especially the road atop the dike that sat between Lake Phelps and the fields. Storms in the fall and winter whipped the lake into an ocean-like frenzy, and this dike was all that sat between the fields and a flood.

October was also the beginning of the corn harvest, most of which was done by women. While they picked, the men plowed the ground behind them, preparing for the next spring's planting. By the end of November, the piles of picked corn were loaded on flatboats and floated to the plantation's four-story barn, where the unshelled ears were stored. Some of them would be shucked during the winter, when there was nothing else to do, but most corn was not shelled until the spring, when merchant barges arrived at the waterfront barn, inside which four oxen pulled a massive cart up and down ramps to all four levels. The scope and efficiency of the Collins corn barn was near-legend throughout the southeast. It was as close as those swamps would ever come to a factory.

December was a time for cleaning buildings, stowing firewood, cutting grass and spreading straw in the fields. It was also time for a hog killing, when as many as a hundred hogs would be slaughtered and the pork stored to feed the slaves. The year then ended with a five-day holiday beginning Christmas Day.

Year in, year out, that was life in the fields. Meanwhile, inside

Slaves dressed in their "Sunday best" watering and plowing the fields.

and around the mansion, a staff of twenty-five house servants kept the Collinses comfortable. Meals were cooked in a detached kitchen building and carried to the house. A staff of gardeners, including Fred Littlejohn, tended the Collinses' three-acre vegetable garden, a fruit orchard of pear, hazelnut and apple trees and a formal flower garden. Inside the house a staff of servants headed by a slave named Luke Davis kept the rooms and their fourteen imported European carpets clean. Two men had the full-time job of keeping the woodhouse full and the home's eight fireplaces glowing. A footman and driver had the singular job of keeping Collins' carriage ready to roll.

There were so many jobs on the plantation—this was, after all, a self-contained community. I collected hundreds of slave names, but I had no idea what most of them actually did. I knew Ishmael Harvey was a shoemaker, saving Collins the cost of hiring outside cobblers to keep his slaves' feet covered. I knew Grace Blount was the Collinses' chief cook. I knew Wellington Roberts was their coachman. But I had only clues to others. A tax list told me Mack Treadwell, at one thousand dollars, was Collins' highest-valued slave in 1839. He must have been an artisan. Dick Blount, a shoemaker, was taxed at nine hundred the same year—a price well beyond what a mere shoemaker would have brought. He must also have had a position of authority on the plantation—he was among the first slaves to arrive on the scene when the Collins boys drowned in the canal, and he was the one who pulled their bodies out along with the overseer.

A thirty-two-year-old slave named Cuffee was worth only two hundred dollars on that 1839 list—he was either sick, hurt or a poor worker. King Junior was valued at nothing, but it was easy to see why—he was listed as "blind and useless" from birth.

One slave who may have been worth more to the Collinses than any other was a man named Joe Welcome. Welcome had done bricklaying for Josiah I in Edenton before coming to Somerset in 1803. He and another slave named Jim Miller did most of the brickwork on Ebenezer Pettigrew's Bonarva plantation as well as building all the brick foundations, chimneys and walkways at Somerset. And, although his name is nowhere to be found on the plaques lining the brick walls of Edenton's downtown St. Paul's Episcopal Church—plaques honoring that town's most storied colonial forefathers—it was Joe Welcome who built those walls. Every time I went back to Edenton to check the courthouse records, I looked at that magnolia-shaded church and thought about how proud Joe would be to see those bricks still standing—as proud as I was to find out he laid them.

The work they did for Collins filled the days of the Somerset slaves. But there was still work they needed to do for themselves. It was on their own time that the slaves grew corn on the fifty-five-acre plot set aside by Collins as the "Negro patch." It was on their own time that they were free to hunt for bear, coons, possums, squirrels, geese, ducks, turkeys and quails. That was to supplement the hogs and chickens they were allowed to raise for themselves and the fish they were allowed to pull from the lake.

153

But even these apparent freedoms actually helped keep Josiah III in control. Both Collins and Pettigrew had commissaries on their plantations. Slaves who followed the rules, who got the crops in on time, earned cash or credits that could be exchanged for goods at these plantation stores.

Each slave had an account, which gave him or her extra incentive to work. Of course the field hands, who had less opportunity to make extra money, had less to do with the store than the skilled artisans. But to the slaves who collected enough money and credits, the store sold food, clothing, skins, mirrors, knives, even fiddles—all treats for slaves who owned almost nothing. They were things to thirst after, even be greedy for. And that made the store's ledger books just another means to punish a slave without beating him. In 1819 Pettigrew handled an unruly slave named David by taking away the slave's "ballance" at the Bonarva store. When another slave named Anthony ran away the same year, Pettigrew took away "this fellows crop." Also the same year, a woman named Amelia "forfeited by outrageous conduct in many ways for 5 yrs her share." What I wouldn't give to find out just what Amelia did.

Collins' supply store was open not only to his slaves, but also to poor whites from surrounding farms, who had no place nearby to shop. Apparently some of Josiah III's slaves did business with these whites as well as with Collins, even though trading between slaves and whites was illegal. In two cases recorded in the Chowan County courthouse—one in 1830 and the other

154

in 1839—white men were indicted for buying and receiving corn from four different Collins slaves.

Early on, there was a strange bond between the slaves and the poor whites. Both were, in their own way, under the yoke of the rich white man. By the time of the Civil War, poor whites around Somerset were urging the blacks to break away from Collins long before the first Union troops set foot on the plantation. It was an odd alliance that broke apart once the slaves were free and competing directly with the poor whites for what little was left after the war.

When it finally came, freedom was just a word to the Somerset slaves. A century after the Emancipation Proclamation, it's still a word that brings a bitter laugh from some blacks. But at least we can grasp the concept. The Somerset slaves hardly had that chance. For almost one hundred years, the Collinses did their best to create a state of mind among their slaves of utter dependency. Crumbs of freedom were issued here and there, but they were all strategic, all aimed at tightening the knots of control. Josiah III extended his reach everywhere, even inside the doors of the church. When it came to chaining his chattel, the Lord was one of Collins' most effective tools.

He gave his slaves a church, the largest building on the plantation—next to his own mansion. But Collins built it out of fear, not faith—fear that his slaves might become too independent following the African-rooted gods or black Methodist preachers they had been allowed when no master was living with them. Nat

Turner, after all, had been fired by the lightning of black religion.

Collins worked hard at prying his slaves from their own worship and turning them into Episcopalians. He hired resident ministers to live at Somerset and conduct daily morning and evening prayer services for the slaves as well as for his own family. Collins himself read the Bible at Sunday services. And the Somerset slaves did become good students, studying catechism and memorizing Scriptures. Dr. Edward Warren was as impressed as a good white Christian could be when Josiah III took him to see the slave services:

> Indeed, it was a constant source of interest to see the negroes flocking to church on Sundays, participating in the services—for they knew every word of the "prayer-book"—and partaking of the holy communion at the same table with their master and the members of his family.

But, according to Warren, even the best of the black Christians he saw would not lay aside their African culture.

> Though rampant Christians, with "the service" upon the tips of their tongues, they still had faith in evil genii, charms, philters, metempsychosis, etc., and they habitually indulged in an infinitude of cabalistic rites and ceremonies, in which the gizzards of chickens, the livers of dogs, the heads of snakes and the tails of lizards played a mysterious but very conspicuous part.

It's hard not to see Warren's bigotry seeping through—the smug white doctor fascinated by the primitive savages. But there's no doubt some of the African in the Somerset slaves did survive. Inbred culture built up over millennia does not fade away in a matter of decades. Neither does the human will of resistance. Try as he might, there was no way Collins could control his slaves as completely as he would have liked. And once a year he actually admitted this: At Christmas.

Every Christmas the Somerset slaves kicked off their five-day holiday by acting out the John Canoe, or "John Koonering," ceremony. The ritual was common in eighteenth-century Jamaica, where an elaborate mumming ceremony was staged. But its roots most likely came from the west coast of Africa, where yam festivals are celebrated with men dressed as sorcerers. As generations passed, many of the African traditions and customs must have faded at Somerset. But the John Koonering was one that lasted. Each Christmas Day, slaves wearing elaborate costumes of rags and animal skins would lead other slaves dressed in their Sunday best onto the porch of Collins' mansion—territory they were forbidden to enter any other day of the year. The rest of the plantation's slaves would follow in a crowd, clapping their hands and dancing as the costumed leaders beat drums and sang a song, demanding a symbolic offering from the master. Again, Dr. Warren, whose idea of music and dancing was a minuet and a quadrille, was on hand to give an amazed firsthand account:

> One of their customs was playing at what they called "John Koonering" . . . on Christmas day. The leading character is the "ragman," whose "get-up" consists of a costume of rags, so ar-

ranged that one end of each hangs loose and dangles; two great ox horns, attached to the skin of a raccoon, which is drawn over the head and face, leaving apertures only for the eyes and mouth; sandals of the skin of some wild "varmint"; several cow or sheep bells or strings of dried goats' horns hanging about their shoulders, and so arranged as to jingle at every movement; and a short stick of seasoned wood, carried in his hands.

The second . . . carried in his hand a small bowl or tin cup, while . . . half a dozen other fellows, each arrayed fantastically in ribbons, rags, and feathers, bear between them several so-called musical instruments or "gumba boxes," which consist of wooden frames covered over with tanned sheepskin. These are usually followed by a motley crowd of all ages, dressed in their ordinary working clothes, which seemingly comes as a guard of honor to the performers.

. . . Coming up to the front door of the "great house," the musicians commenced to beat their gumba-boxes violently, while characters No. 1 and No. 2 enter upon a dance of the most extraordinary character—a combination of bodily contortions, flings, kicks, gyrations, and antics of every imaginable description, seemingly acting as partners, and yet each trying to excel the other . . . while the whole crowd joined in the chorus, shouting and clapping their hands in the wildest glee.

The poor doctor was shaken. And I'm not sure Collins felt any calmer. I could see him reluctantly stepping forward and dropping a coin in the slaves' cup, as he did each year. And I could see the slaves moving on to each of the other white residences on the estate—the tutor's rooms, the parson's study, the overseer's house—making the same demand of each of them. As quaint as it may have seemed to the Collinses, they had to be slightly disturbed to feel the strange power and unreined energy of their slaves—even if for only one day a year.

For all Collins' efforts at keeping the slave families together, there was an innate instability about their lives that he could never remove. Their fate on earth, after all, was out of their hands—a point that was brutally brought home in 1839. That was the year Josiah II died. His will dictated the equal division of his slaves among his eight children. Josiah III did the dividing, as coldly and mathematically as he counted bushels of his corn. He inventoried all his Somerset and Edenton slaves, noting which had belonged to his father. Then he assigned a probate value to each of those slaves, divided them into eight equal lots, assigned one lot to each of his brothers and sisters, then bought their lots of slaves from them, selling some in turn to other owners. He tried to keep slave children with parents, but slave siblings, grandparents and grandchildren were torn apart. Slaves who had spent their lives in Edenton and Somerset were suddenly shipped to other owners and other homes. One group of eighty-one was torn from its relatives and ended up in Marengo County, Alabama, never to be heard of at Somerset again.

Surrounded by uncertainty, the Somerset slaves still managed to build stability from within, a stability founded on their families—the only things they could really call their own. Because the family was so important, the slaves were careful about choosing mates and dead serious about keeping them. Babies were often born before marriage, but these were a result of practical "trying out" of mates rather than simple promiscuity. Most un-wed parents on the plantation eventually married, and their vows were earnest. There is no evidence that a divorce ever occurred among the slaves at Somerset. And the owners apparently realized how much marriage meant to their slaves. Ebenezer Pettigrew wrote of a recently married friend: "Miss Lowther, as the negroes say, has tied a knot with her tongue which she can't untie with her teeth."

So isolated, so alone, drawn totally unto themselves. Except for the few slaves who were allowed to visit their relatives in Edenton during Christmas, the Somerset blacks rarely stepped off their plantation except to visit the one next door. Still, with the steady flow of new purchases moving onto the plantation, as well as the community of Pettigrew slaves next door, there was enough "new stock" that the Somerset slaves were always able to find mates outside their own families. Incest was not a necessity at Somerset.

As rumors of war began to fly, the isolation got worse. Uriah Bennett remembered: "For months and months at a time we were never allowed off the farm. Sometimes we would get as far as the gate and peep over. We were told that if we got outside the Padirollers would get us."

Patrollers. As war neared, slaves on many plantations began to flee, tantalized by the very mention of freedom. Slave patrols became common, and word quickly spread among blacks that the "padirollers" were more brutal than any overseer. Fear was in the air.

And confusion. The Somerset slaves may have been heart-

160

ened to see the Union soldiers arrive, but when one of the blue-jacketed soldiers threw Lovey Harvey—the thirty-five-year-old wife of Davidson Harvey and the mother of four children—in the cook house and raped her at gun point, the blacks had to have questions about "liberation." They would have had even more questions if they had heard the words penned by a Union soldier camped in North Carolina in 1862. He wrote home to some abolitionist friends in Boston: "If you could see the greasy dirty black paws that handle our food," he wrote, "you would alter your tune."

Fred Littlejohn—who was called "Fred Elsy" by the minister who wrote Collins about the "defiant" slave who helped the Yankees steal horses—had no doubt whose side he was on. But many of the others weren't so sure. The slave narratives collected in the 1930s from blacks who had been on other North Carolina plantations gave me a glimpse into attitudes about slaveowners and about Yankees. As I read them, I realized these former slaves were facing white interviewers in the climate of the Ku Klux Klan, the segregated South. They most likely told the white people what they thought they wanted to hear. But, in any case, their attitudes are both curious and compelling.

"I haven't anything to say against slavery," said Simuel Riddick, who had been owned in Perquimans County, north of Somerset. "My old folks put my clothes on me when I was a boy. They gave me shoes and stockings and put them on me when I was a little boy. I loved them and I can't go against them in anything. There were things I did not like about slavery on some plantations, whuppin' and sellin' parents and children from each other, but I haven't much to say. I was treated good."

Blount Baker, who had been a slave in Wilson County, didn't like what he saw of the Union troops:

We ain't seed no Yankees 'cept a few huntin' Rebs. Dey talks mean ter us an' one of dem says dat we niggers am de cause of de war. "Sir," I says, "folks what am a wantin' a war can always find a cause." He kicks me in de seat of de pants fer dat, so I hushes.

A woman named Mary Anderson vividly recalled the emotion and turmoil the day the Yankees arrived on the Wake County plantation where she was a slave:

162

Nobody was working and slaves were walking over the grove in every direction. At nine o'clock all the slaves gathered at the great house and marster and missus came out on the porch and stood side by side. You could hear a pin drop everything was so quiet. Then marster said, "Good morning," and missus said, "Good morning, children." They were both crying. Then marster said, "Men, women and children, you are free. You are no longer my slaves. The Yankees will soon be here."

Marster and missus then went into the house, got two large arm chairs, put them on the porch facing the avenue and sat down side by side and remained there watching.

In about an hour there was one of the blackest clouds coming up the avenue from the main road. It was the Yankee soldiers, they finally filled the mile long avenue reaching from marster's house to the main Louisburg road and spread out over the mile square grove. The mounted men dismounted. The footmen stacked their shining guns and began to build fires and cook. They called the slaves, saying, "You are free." Slaves were whooping and laughing and acting like they were crazy. Yankee soldiers were shaking hands with the Negroes and calling them Sam, Dinah, Sarah and asking them questions. They busted the door to the smoke house and got all the hams. They went to the icehouse and got several barrels of brandy, and such a time.

The Negroes and Yankees were cooking and eating together. The Yankees told them to come on and join them, they were free. Marster and missus sat on the porch and they were so humble no Yankee bothered anything in the great house. The slaves were awfully excited. The Yankees stayed there, cooked, ate, drank and played music until about night, then a bugle began to blow and you never saw such getting on horses and lining up in your life. In a few minutes they began to march, leaving the grove which was soon as silent as a grave yard . . .

When they left the country, lot of the slaves went with them and soon there were none of marster's slaves left . . . They wandered around for a year from place to place, fed and working most of the time at some other slave owner's plantation and getting more homesick every day.

The second year after the surrender our marster and missus got on their carriages and went and looked up all the Negroes they heard of who ever belonged to them. Some who went off with the Yankees were never heard of again. When marster and missus found any of theirs they would say, "Well, come on back home. . . ."

When they got back marster would say, "Well, you have come back home have you?" And the Negroes would say, "Yes, marster." Most all spoke of them as missus and marster as they did before the surrender, and getting back home was the greatest pleasure of all.

Getting back home. That was all the Somerset slaves had on their minds once they were torn from their families and taken "up country" by Collins in 1862. I could only imagine the details of the forced march they took from Somerset to Hurry Scurry. I could only imagine the unfathomable strength they must have

163

had to endure the pain and heartache of this sudden separation, on top of the degradation and oppression they dealt with each day of their lives. Collins was no longer concerned with keeping family units intact. He was scrambling for his economic life now, leaving able-bodied men and the elderly at Somerset, while taking mostly women and children inland and hiring out what men he brought with him. The fiber of the slave families was ripped as never before, with elders and husbands separated from women and children.

And still they endured, clinging to the hope that they would someday be brought back together at Somerset, the only world they knew. Most of them waited, working at the "up country" railroad, hospital and farm jobs for which Collins hired them out. But one group of younger slaves couldn't wait. They were some of Fred Littlejohn's family—two nieces, a nephew, his twenty-one-year-old daughter Ruth and his sixteen-year-old son Alfred. My great-grandpa Alfred. On June 1, 1863—five months after the Emancipation Proclamation took effect—those five children slipped away from Hurry Scurry, headed east toward Somerset.

The fear they must have felt, slipping through the woods, keeping away from the roads, hiding and sleeping by day, running at night, stealing fruit from orchards along the way, never sure if a slave patrol might be around the next ridge. Or a farmer ready to do his duty to the Confederacy.

Collins knew there was only one route through the hills that rolled east toward Somerset, and he knew that route went through the town of Tarboro. When he realized the children were gone, he wrote ahead to a friend, who posted notices in Tarboro and Rocky Mount offering a hundred dollars reward for each of the runaways. He also hired two slave catchers, who were posted along the main road south of Tarboro.

On June 15, two of the girls were caught by a man named E. Duncan McNara, who wrote Collins that he had turned them over to Collins' brutal Hurry Scurry overseer, a man named Lloyd Bateman:

> . . . delivered two girls to Bateman. My only fear is that Bateman will be too severe with those negroes for I was there yesterday and he seemed very angry with them. He said he already struck one two-hundred.

165

Whipping. That's what the war had brought Collins to.

By June 19, the other three runaway children were caught. When asked where they were headed, they simply answered, "Home."

Josiah Collins III was not standing on any front porch telling his slaves they were free. He was hiding in the hills, holding onto as much of his black property as he could. But he couldn't keep the slaves back at Somerset from testing the limits of the "freedom" that was in the air. The overseer, a man named George Spruill, had a hard time ordering the slaves to work after Yankee soldiers visited the plantation in the spring of 1863 and "told the Negroes they were free & could do as they pleased." Most of them stayed, but they insisted on working only for wages. When Spruill refused to pay the black mill hands, the mill closed down. When he refused to pay the field hands, they let the farm go to weed during the summer, while they tended the crops in their own patches. The winter was rougher, since they had to rely on Spruill to give them corn from the plantation's barns.

One young slave named James Augustus was lured by the Yankees' words, moving west to the town of Plymouth. But he came home after just a few weeks, complaining that the Federals had "made him work very hard and fed him badly," according to a letter written to Collins in the spring of 1863. That summer, wrote Spruill, "the other negroes behave much better since Jim's return. They have all gone to work on the farm."

But they didn't work long, not while Collins' kingdom was crumbling around them. By the spring of 1863, the property was easy prey for looters. In the same letter that described Jim's return, Spruill told Collins what was happening to his home:

> [Neighboring poor whites] supplied themselves with corn from the plantation & several young horses. The garden once so beautiful was torn and trampled down. The house was maliciously abused and the libraries were carted away to Plymouth & from thence transferred to Yankeedom. The furniture, the "Buffs" have in a great measure divided among themselves. Mr. Warren Ambrose a poor white farmer it is said, has furnished his house to a most extravagant state. They have taken away all the horses, mules, cattle, hogs & sheep, except very few.

As the chaos got worse, Spruill got more desperate. He began paying the slaves with hogs and cattle. He began "talking to them." "By those means," he wrote Collins, "i have kept them on the lake."

But by May, the slaves were referring to their owner as "Old Collins." "They does not cear for you Collins at all," wrote Spruill. The slaves were "farming on their own rule," he wrote. By then, the few hogs that had not been given to the slaves were rooting for themselves in the woods.

In June, Collins died.

Over the next two years, Collins' widow did all she could to hold onto her husband's slaves. She scrambled to hire them out, to raise money to help pay for the high cost of keeping them alive. But the railroads, farmers and Confederate hospitals to whom she hired her slaves were also feeling the squeeze of the war. By the end of 1864, most of them hadn't paid her the money she was promised and she was forced to sell two horses for twelve hundred dollars, a pair of mules for four thousand, and a carriage and harness for six hundred—all to pay her mounting debts. Also, in desperation, she sold a slave named Nelly—for twenty-one hundred dollars.

The following year was even worse. Mules and slaves were not enough. Now Mary Collins was forced to part with her precious silver, specifically a silver plate that she sold for eleven thousand dollars—five times the price of Nelly.

In April 1865—more than two years after the Emancipation Proclamation—the war ended and the slaves at Hurry Scurry

167

were freed. They walked home—devastated, starving, stealing—
arriving to weep with relatives they hadn't seen for more than
two years. Collins' son George also returned with his brother
Arthur and his mother. He refused to pay people he still considered his slaves, and the only reason the blacks stayed at Somerset through that year was to harvest the corn they had planted
for themselves in the spring. When Josiah IV took over the
plantation that winter and refused to rent land to the blacks,
they left Somerset, this time for good. Some cut all ties, moving
to Virginia and farther north. But most settled in the surrounding area. Some farmed. Others built homes in the swamps, cutting cypress shingles for a living, as they had done for Collins for
nothing.

Luke Davis stayed on at Somerset after most of the others had
left. He worked "from daybreak until long after night fall, sometimes going without his dinner," wrote one of the Collinses. But
even Luke eventually left. The plantation seemed "lonesome,"
he told the Collinses. His family was "unhappy." The only reason he had stayed longer than most of the former slaves, he told
his former masters, wrote George Collins, was "because he
seems to be really sorry for us."

That was how it ended for the slaves at Somerset. It had begun
with thirty or so American-born slaves in 1785, who were joined
by eighty Africans in 1786. It lasted eighty years and four generations. The first slaves knew life before the Lake Phelps swamps.
The last knew life beyond them. But in between there were more

than a hundred men, women and children who were born and died without ever knowing a day when they were not a Somerset slave. I couldn't have understood the enormity of that fact if I hadn't gathered, one by one, the names of those people. And, after finding several books on slave-naming patterns, I was able to learn the meanings of most of those names.

First, those books established that slaves did not always take the surname of their last master. Instead, they more often kept the last names of their original owner. Although Nat Turner was sold by Benjamin Turner to Putnam Moore, then was passed on to Joseph Travis, he was still Nat Turner when he was hanged. Elsy Littlejohn was sold to Josiah Collins, but she remained a Littlejohn—although her son Fred was called Fred *Elsy* by an overseer who had problems telling him apart from another Fred.

It was convenient for the overseer to call Fred Elsy. That was another major factor in naming—convenience. While the slaves kept their original owners' names, they were often the only ones to use those names. Their current owners often simply called them by their first name or by a handy last name the owner or overseer made up for easy identification. Collins called one slave who tended the hogs Jack Swine. After Jack lost a leg, he was called Doctor Jack. His real name was Jack Sawyer.

Things got stickier for the owners when several slaves had the same first name. In 1839 there were five Peters at Somerset. Rather than taking the time to find how those men were called among their fellow slaves, the owner or overseers tagged them with their own labels, none of which were the names the slaves used among themselves.

In one book on slave names, written by a man named Eugene D. Genovese, the silliness of some names used by the white owners was described:

> Few pompous, classical or comical names imposed by slave owners, such as Caesar, Cato and Pompey, survived the war. The freedmen divested themselves of these names so quickly that one wonders if they [slaves] had ever used them among themselves in the quarters.

Did the slave whom Pettigrew called Pompey call himself by that name?

I knew where my own name came from—Elsy and Peter had brought it with them from Edenton to Somerset. Somewhere further back, of course, I was African. But that didn't matter now. The pages and pages of family trees I had drawn trying to sort out the families of Somerset slaves now took on a different purpose. I had begun my search looking for my own roots. They had turned out to be more extensive than I ever dreamed. Now I needed to take those roots forward, to find what they all grew into.

I knew now how the Littlejohns grew. Peter and Elsy had eleven children before they were done, and eighteen grandchildren by 1865. They were a good investment for Collins. He paid less than two hundred dollars each for Elsy and the six children she brought with her to Somerset. For that sum—about thirteen hundred dollars—he eventually ended up with thirty-one slaves. That figures out to less than fifty dollars a person. No wonder Collins was anti-abolition.

It was the fall of 1984. Ronald Reagan had been elected to a second presidential term. Civil rights had become a thinly disguised joke. But my focus was broader. I wasn't just looking back at twenty years. I was now looking back at centuries. It had been seven years since I had first sat down with my mother. I now knew what "over de river" really meant. The family I had gone after had blossomed into something larger than I'd ever imagined. So many slaves at Somerset were my kin. By traveling backward I had found an entire community of relatives I never knew existed—a group of people who had been torn from the only home they ever knew and had the strength to finally make it back. I had learned all I could about who they were—all except what became of them once they were free.

For almost a century, Somerset was a self-contained pod of people, one of hundreds of pods like it throughout the South. When those pods burst in 1865, seeds like the one that spawned me were scattered in the wind. I had to find the seeds that had mixed with mine—the Somerset sisters and brothers I knew were out there. It was time to work forward now, to close the circle.

CONNECTING

I'd like to have something on the slave experience."

He didn't mean anything by it, but the way Bill Edwards spoke those words, he could have been an office manager ordering up a f!e. "Something on the slave experience." The phrase rang hard. So curt, so cold.

It was a warm spring morning in 1984, and Edwards was talking to me about something he called Founders Day. Edwards was the Somerset Place site manager, and he was planning the event for the next month. It would be a kind of May fair. There would be arts and crafts and historical exhibitions, all on the plantation grounds, he said. A day of celebration at Somerset. And he wondered if I'd like to set up a display of my study.

Until then everything I'd done had been purely personal. All

my results and my research, my diagrams and notes—the stuff of
my ancestors' story—were bulging from the drawers and shelves
in my den. I'd shared them at a few meetings with genealogists
and I'd showed them at church. But here was a chance to open
them to the public, at Somerset itself. I wasn't quite sure exactly
what this Founders Day event was going to be, but I was ready to
be a part of it.

And I was going to make it good. I went to the art supply
store, bought cardboard paper and matting, pens and pencils,
went home and drew charts and maps. I made lists of the twenty-
one Littlejohn-linked slave family lines I'd traced at Somerset. I
even got an artist to draw a map of North Carolina, plotting the
trail the slaves had hiked from Somerset to Hurry Scurry and
back.

The day came, and I packed the car with my charts, picked up
my mother and headed toward Somerset. For Mother, this was a
special trip. By now she was almost as much a part of this journey as I was. She was so proud, so eager to let the world know
she was a Littlejohn, and now was her big chance. It was all she
could talk about on the drive down.

The heat was blistering by the time we reached the plantation.
As we looked for Edwards, I noticed other people setting up
their own displays under the shade of the oaks or inside the air-
conditioned visitors center. There were a couple of can-
dlemakers, a man making brooms, two men making wooden
shingles. All of them were white. Out on the lawn was a barbecue

grill set up by the local volunteer fire department. The firemen were all white, too. So were the spectators who were already beginning to trickle across the lawn.

We found Edwards, and he led us to the spot he'd set aside for me. The kitchen. This was the outbuilding where the slaves had cooked Josiah Collins' food. This was the room where Lovey Harvey had been raped. It was not air-conditioned, like the visitors center. It had no wiring, no outlets to plug in a fan. Just a table, two chairs, and the hot, sullen mid-morning air.

We sat inside that stifling room, my seventy-seven-year-old mother and I, watching white people come and go past the door, white people who weren't even interested in the displays their own kind had set up, much less a black woman's charts about her slave ancestors. Most had come for the barbecue. They paid little attention to us. Some glanced in, then kept moving. Some probably thought we worked there. Hired help.

It was a humiliating day—humiliating most of all to see my mother, so hopeful when we had arrived, now baking in this sweatbox as people walked past who didn't care who she was or why she was here—why she was anywhere. By the time we packed the car and headed home, I realized that blacks had nothing to do with this place. Somerset had nothing to do with us, and neither did we have anything to do with it. Blacks didn't come out for this special day. Nor did we come out any other day. Why would we? To take a tour of the Collins mansion? I looked at those white men cutting shingles for fun, and thought

175

about the slaves who had done nothing here but slice cypress all their lives, day in and day out. For the descendants of those slaves, shingle-making was a heritage. For these white men, it was a hobby.

The whole site was so thin, so empty, so devoid of feeling. And it was easy to see why—the lifeblood of this plantation had been the slaves, not the whites. Yes, a handful of white people lived in that fine house and controlled the farm, but the fabric, the texture, the resonance of this lakefront land came from the hundreds of black people who lived here. We were Somerset Place, not an empty mansion and a slim brochure.

I wasn't really surprised to see no blacks at Edwards' event. I'd already gotten a sense of the distance Somerset descendants had put between themselves and the plantation—not in miles but in their minds. Some had done it consciously, others without even realizing it. But most of the black people living in the small houses along the drainage ditches that now bound what was once the west end of Collins' estate no longer even referred to Somerset by name. They recalled their grandparents talking about where they'd come from—grandparents who had been Somerset slaves. But they didn't mention slavery nor did they mention Somerset.

"Yes," people would tell me, "our family comes from over on Western Farm," not realizing—or recognizing—that Western Farm was simply a designated section of the vastness that was Somerset.

"Oh yeah," others would say, "we come from up on Sheppard Farm."

Or, "Uh huh, I used to hear talk about our people coming from over on Magnolia."

Sheppard was another section of Somerset. Magnolia was part of the Pettigrew plantation. They were all pieces of the frame that bound Somerset, but over the years—whether by design or simply by the withering of facts that comes with the passage of time—the big picture had been lost. What was left were fragments of memories about fragments of the plantations. No wonder there was little interest among blacks in the Somerset site. Not only was it run by whites, but it had been disowned by blacks.

And why not? Most black people around Creswell were too busy just getting by to worry about things like heritage and history. Who's got time for the past when the present is squeezing in on all sides, when the rain rips through the plastic tacked on the side window, when the mosquitoes hover in clouds off the swamp water in the front yard ditch and the closest thing you've got to transportation is the car sitting over in those weeds, rusted to the color of the clay it's stuck in.

There are fewer than fifteen thousand people living in Washington County. Four hundred and twenty-six of them live in Creswell: Two hundred and sixty-seven whites, one hundred and fifty-five blacks, two Indians and two "others," according to the county records. The county's official median per capita income is nine thousand nine hundred dollars. For blacks, it is lower, though the county can't say just how much. They don't keep those figures, says the clerk at the county manager's office. They don't keep those figures for Creswell either, but it's a good bet that Creswell's blacks bottom out on the median income scale.

Clearly, Somerset was not on most people's minds when I began knocking on doors that summer of 1984. Still, I was out to put it there. I drove the hot dusty roads through the countryside around Creswell, checking mailboxes for names I'd recognize, knocking on doors, inviting myself up on porches, explaining to puzzled faces what I had been doing for the last seven years and asking them if they'd mind chatting a bit. Some minded. More than a few reacted like the gray-haired woman who gathered her grandson into her arms, refused to look at me and would say only, "Don't know nothin' 'bout that place. *Nothin'.*"

There were some who got nervous when I pulled out a pen and pad. They were real comfortable when we were just talking, but as soon as I started writing, they'd tighten up, turn silent or suddenly tell me, "I think the person you really need to talk to is down the road a bit." I'd listen to the words and I could see the tension in the eyes as a finger pointed toward the treeline.

Still, I had an easier time of it than the white historians who had come through these parts over the years, trying to collect information for this study or that. The people sitting on these porches were, on the whole, elderly black women. The histori-

178

ans were white, usually male, with about as much chance of getting a meaningful interview as a slaveowner might have had interviewing a slave. I, on the other hand, was black, a woman and, most of all, I had the name. All I had to do was mention the Littlejohn name, and folks would come out from behind screen doors, neighbors would appear from behind fences, somebody would stroll down from the house up the road. They'd offer me food, ask me inside for some iced tea or Kool-Aid, pull out photographs, give me addresses and phone numbers of their children who had moved away and when they were done they'd point me to so-and-so up the road, whose granddaddy, they believed, did work over on Western Farm.

Spruills, Baums, Bennetts, Cabarruses. All alive and in the flesh. After being submerged for so long among papers and documents of long-dead people, I was finally back in the land of the living.

A community—nothing more than a cluster of homes—had sprung up at the edge of what had been Western Farm. They called it Cherry, and from the porches of those houses you could look across the fields and see the shadowy wall of Somerset cypresses in the distance. The land in between had long been divided up and sold off. Most of it was now owned by a white Davenport family, descendants of former overseers at Somerset and Bonarva. It was ironic that the Collinses' overseers and not the Collinses themselves ended up with all that land—poorer whites taking over what the rich man had left behind. During the earlier part of this century, local blacks were hired to work in those fields, but come harvest time migrant workers arrived to help bring in the crops. In Poppa Littlejohn's day, those workers had been blacks from further south, field hands and drifters who made their way up the East Coast, guided by the seasons. These were the people Poppa had put up in the extra rooms in his Columbia house. But most local blacks steered away from the migrants, in the same way I'd seen New York City blacks sneer at their country cousins from the South. Everybody needs someone to feel a bit above, I guess. By the time I began driving the roads around Cherry and Creswell, the black migrants were gone, but another group had taken their place: Cubans, up from Florida.

The first summer I'd been at Somerset I'd seen them arrive, dropped off by bus and moving into a group of tin-topped shacks just down the road from the cypress-lined entrance. I didn't know it then, but I later found out those shacks sat a few feet from the spot where Collins' enormous canal-front barn had once stood. The Cubans who walked into the shacks were worn and ragged. Beaten in every sense of the word. At dawn they went into the fields—men, women and children. At sunset they came back to the shacks. And in the dusky time between sunset and darkness, they'd all walk over to the historic site, sitting on the benches in the shade and watching the mist rise over the empty stillness of the park grounds. I'd be there some of those evenings, and I tried talking to the women. But I couldn't. They spoke no English, and I spoke no Spanish.

Isolated, alone and choiceless: These Cubans were little more than modern slaves. The shacks they lived in were actually worse than the Collins' slave quarters had been. The slave quarters at least had fireplaces and the breezes off the lake. These shacks were hot, cramped, dusty, with no fireplaces and few windows. They were nothing more than roofs and walls—the roofs leaked, and the walls were falling in. Like Collins' chattel, these Cuban people were cut off from the world beyond the fields they worked in. They had no transportation, Creswell was a hot five-mile walk away, and what was there for them if they went? They had no money to speak of. They worked in the fields, totally at the whim of the landowners who paid them whatever wages they pleased. When their day was done, they simply sat and waited for night to fall, as much prisoners of the plantation as my ancestors had been.

But most blacks in these parts knew nothing of the details of Somerset and its slavery. Those who did kept what they knew locked deep in their subconscious. There were only two blacks in the area—two—who had anything to do with that plantation: my mother's cousin, Odessa Cabarrus, and her cousin, Elsie.

Mother had mentioned Odessa's name many times over the years, but I'd never met her until that summer day I drove to her home, out past Cherry. Everybody said Odessa lived with her cousin, out by a chicken farm west of Cherry. Just look for the chicken farm, everybody said. So I went the way they pointed, and the hardtop gave way to dirt road. The dust billowed up in my rearview mirror, and bushes scraped the sides of my car.

There was no building in sight, but after a while I knew I was getting close. I didn't have to look for any chicken farm—I could smell it.

Cousin Odessa's house was just beyond the henhouses. Turned out the chickens were just a landmark. They belonged to a white man, not to her. Odessa lived in a neat, whitewashed, two-story house smothered in flowers. Odessa loved flowers and had them growing everywhere around the house, outside and in. Her husband was dead, but Odessa still worked, cleaning houses for white families and as a part-time maid at the school over in Creswell now that she was too old to keep her job there full time. She'd been a maid at the school for as long as anyone could remember.

She was a tall woman, thin, fair-skinned. Thick glasses. She was in her late-seventies, same as my mother. And sure enough, her cousin Ernest, in his sixties, was right there with her. So was a granddaughter, who was visiting with Odessa during the semester break at Elizabeth City State University. "Yeah," said Ernest, "we raised us some good children." He said it with real pride, just as if he'd raised the girl, not Odessa.

Odessa was inside frying some fish for lunch when I came by. And she had some corn bread in the oven, the kind of food I don't get back in Portsmouth. Of course she asked me to pull up a chair. That's the way country people and the elderly always do it. That's their greeting, their way of welcome: Sit down and have a bite to eat.

I had questions for Odessa, questions about her own Hortin family line—the descendants of Yellowman Dave. She helped clear up a little confusion about the first generation born free, about which was Daniel Hortin and which was David. But it was when she got to talking about the Cabarruses that things got real interesting. I mentioned Somerset Place, and she nodded her head.

Cousin Odessa told me how every Christmas she would go over to the plantation, to the Collins mansion itself. She'd help decorate for the holiday open house they had there each year. It was a white event, both the decorating and the open house. Odessa was almost always the only black there, but she didn't feel out of place. The reason was simple, she explained.

"My great-great-grandmother died in one of those rooms up there," she said.

She was talking about Charlotte Cabarrus, Collins' free nurse-maid. Odessa was telling me she and the rest of the Cabarrus side of her family were descendants of Charlotte Cabarrus. Odessa was proud to go into the house where her great-great-grandmother had worked, to walk into the room where she had slept. That's why she had no problem identifying with Somerset —there was no slave shadow hanging over her.

But she was wrong. Charlotte Cabarrus was nobody's great-great-grandmother. She never had a child. All the Cabarruses who had children at Somerset were field families. The records left no doubt. And I had the records in my hand.

183

I pointed it all out, as gently as I could. No outsider could have told Cousin Odessa what I was telling her. But I was blood kin. My mother's grandmother and Odessa's grandfather were brother and sister. So she listened. And she sat, not saying a word. She cut me a look like, "Maybe she's right, and maybe she's not." She didn't nod or shake her head. She just looked. You take something people have believed all their lives, something they've always assumed to be true, and suddenly you tell them it's not so, well, it's bound to shake them up, especially when it comes to family. How easy is it to accept that someone else knows more about your family than you do? What does that do to your sense of self? When I left that day, Odessa was nice as could be, but I'm not sure she'd changed her mind about Charlotte. Even now, I still run into Cabarruses who talk about their grandmother dying up in that house over at Somerset. People believe what they want to—or, when it comes to their sense of self, what they have to.

My cousin Odessa had every reason to believe Charlotte was her ancestor. She was light-skinned, just as Charlotte had been. Most of the Cabarruses were fair-skinned—the badge of a house servant. The Littlejohns, on the other hand, were tall, dark, heavy people—field hands. Genes told the story back when Collins was in charge, and genes don't fade in a century. Driving the roads of Creswell, I could just glance at a person and guess what his slave ancestors' job had been.

It was harder figuring out just what some of the descendants were doing now. Odessa had worked most of her life as a maid over at the Creswell school. Most of the men and women I talked to worked on the farms around town. But now most were old and retired, living on Social Security. The younger ones with education or skills moved away to a bigger place with better jobs. Those that stayed found what work they could, on the few farms hiring help or at this small business or that. Most went on welfare—they say most of the economy around those parts comes through the mail. And then there are the scattered entrepreneurs like the ones who worked the trailer by the Spruill house.

Two ladies—both of them Spruill descendants—were sitting on the front porch of the house when I walked up. It was a small house, green, set back from a dirt driveway just inside town, with a trailer beside it. Trailers are everywhere in a little town like Creswell, and this one looked no different from most—rusty, weeds growing up around the edges—except it was busy. As I sat talking with the ladies, I watched a steady stream of people—all men—climbing in and out of the trailer's rickety metal door. A stuffed sofa was sitting in the weeds outside the door, and two or three people at a time would be sitting on it, waiting like patients at a dentist's office. There was a little grill going, with a few skinny pieces of chicken barbecuing on it. Nobody seemed to be paying much mind to the chicken. The men on the sofa would just sit awhile, then, when someone would come out the trailer door, one of them would get up and go on in.

There was one man who kept stepping out of the trailer, a huge man, fair-skinned and fat, with his stomach just sagging down over his trousers. He'd step out from the dark insides of that trailer, squint at the sunlight, take a few deep breaths, maybe stroll a few steps in the yard, then go on back inside. As I sat talking with the ladies, I couldn't keep my eyes off the trailer and the fat man and that metal door just banging open and shut over and over again. The Spruill ladies didn't pay any of it any mind. They didn't even look in that direction.

Then it suddenly hit me what I was watching. This had to be a nip joint, a shot house. They were selling liquor or beer or what have you inside that rusty little trailer. And the big man was the boss, the back-room barkeep. I didn't need to ask the ladies what was going on, or why they weren't paying it any mind. That was business as usual over there in the side yard. Didn't have a thing to do with them sitting on the porch.

The ladies were Spruills, not related directly to my father's family line. They were not Spruills from Somerset. This was Spruill land all around them, they said, waving at the ragged pines rimming their lot.

"You see aaaaalllll this land," said one of the ladies, leaning forward in her chair. "Aaaaalllll this land used to belong to Demp Spruill. And when he died, he gave it all to Allan."

Demp Spruill—that would be Dempsey Spruill, who had been a white overseer for the Pettigrews. He owned a little farm of his own, over on the other side of Bonarva. He was no big landowner, but you didn't have to have much to have a slave, and Spruill had a few. One of them was Allan Spruill. I'd seen Allan Spruill's name on the register at St. David's Church, the Pettigrew plantation chapel. St. David's was a white people's church, and I was stunned to find records of blacks who continued to attend even after they were set free. Many of them were even buried there, in unmarked graves. Dozens of churches sprang up around plantations after the war, opened by former slaves who were now free to worship together. They called them bush churches, and there were two right here in Creswell. Yet there were blacks who kept going to church with their former masters. Why?

The answer was simple. All I had to do was check back to what these former slaves' jobs had been when they were on the plantation. All of them had been house servants. They were the slaves who accompanied their masters to church, sitting in the rear while their owners and families worshiped at the front. When the war ended, they still went to the same church and worshiped the same God they had when they were slaves. No one had emancipated their identification with their owners. No one had unlocked their faith in their masters' Lord.

Allan Spruill had been one of those slaves, a house servant on Dempsey Spruill's property. And his descendants sitting on that Creswell porch made a point of saying that Demp had given his black slave this land. They were implying that Allan Spruill was Demp's son. For them, this was a twisted point of pride, the same yearning for the status of West Indian connections that my aunt Dot had had up in New York.

But the Spruill ladies were wrong. Allan Spruill did come into that land, but it was no gift. I found a deed in the Tyrrell County courthouse, dated in the 1880s, showing Allan Spruill's purchase of some land east of Somerset. He paid for it. Less romantic than the ladies' version. But true.

That's the thing about stories. Everybody has one, and most aren't about to let facts get in the way. Some are told so often they become almost parables. Like the blood-in-the-wood, for example.

The first time I heard this one was when I was sitting on Mattie Littlejohn's porch. Mattie was eighty-seven, and her son Cliff was sitting with us. Cliff was in his sixties. I mentioned finding that his uncle Charles Littlejohn had died by drowning in 1936, and Cliff perked up.

"Yeah," he said, "I remember when he died. His body stayed in the water so long that when they got it out it was all puffed up and eaten by fish. All they could do was put him in a little box and set it out on his porch. The blood just dripped out of that box until they took it away and buried him. And for twenty years after that, every time it rained, blood would come up out of the wood on that porch."

What a neat story, I thought. But true? I asked the next person I talked to about it. And the woman just laughed. "He said *what?*" She sat back in her chair, shook her head and chuckled.

"Look, that boy's been drunk for fifty years. *He* mighta seen blood coming out of that porch, but nobody else did."

I thought, God, this is crazy. This is great. Mad. Wonderful. They're so sure of their stories. Then, a while later, I was talking on the phone to Dave Hortin, a direct descendant of Yellowman Dave. Hortin was seventy now, living up in Maryland. He left Creswell in the 1930s. But he remembered playing around the big Somerset barn when he was a little boy, and he got to talking about it.

"Yeah," he said, "that old barn still had the hooks in it, big metal hooks, where they used to put up the slaves' arms."

Uh-huh, I thought. As far as I knew, the hooks were used to tie horses, not slaves. But I let him go on.

"Yes, they used to put the slaves' arms up in those hooks, and they'd beat them, beat them till they bled. And every time it rained . . ."

I couldn't believe it.

". . . you'd see the blood coming back up through the wood."

Okay. One thing I knew for certain. There sure enough must have been some blood coming up through some wood somewhere around these swamps.

True or not, there was a richness to the stories I heard, the tales of family and friends coming and going, some staying their whole lives in the house they were born in, others growing up and leaving, moving west and north. I wanted to talk to them all,

Elijah Honeyblue, born in 1860 at Somerset Place, was the son of Lawrence Honeyblue, an artisan on the plantation. Elijah married Judith Littlejohn, daughter of Fred Littlejohn.

even the ones who left. I got phone numbers, and I called. And their reactions were as different as the people whose doors I knocked on. Some were like Clara Owens, granddaughter of Alpheus Littlejohn, who was Great-grandpa Alfred's brother. Clara had taught school for a long time in the North, then she had moved back to Carolina, to Williamston, sixty miles west of Creswell. "I don't feel comfortable talking about slavery," she told me when I asked about Somerset. "It's too painful. It makes me angry."

It was easy to understand Clara's feelings. She had broken the cycle. She was educated, a professional. Why dredge up the shameful past? But then there were people like William Honeyblue, who felt a little differently. He lived in Williamston, and he was what you might call a success, too—he was that city's mayor pro tem. He was also the grandson of Elijah Honeyblue, a Somerset house servant who had married Judith Littlejohn.

William Honeyblue was eager to help. He knew his grandfa-

Mouring Dickerson married Alpheus Littlejohn, son of Fred Littlejohn.

ther had been a slave. He even had a photograph of him, which he pulled from his album. He sent it to me, along with the story he had heard when he was young about his grandparents struggling back to Somerset from Hurry Scurry after the end of the war, about a white farmer putting his dogs on the hungry slaves trudging home just for eating an apple from his tree.

It's hard to say exactly when the idea set in—I guess it had been deep inside me from the beginning, surfacing by degrees as I went along—but by the end of 1984 I knew we were going to have a homecoming. That's how simply I put it when I walked into Larry Misenheimer's office in January of 1985. Misenheimer was the state's head of historic sites with the Department of Cultural Resources in Raleigh. By then, I had received a grant from the state to spend a week studying papers in the State Archives and copying them for researchers' use at Somerset. I was in his office one day that month, and the words just came out of my mouth:

"We are going to have a homecoming of the descendants of Somerset Place," I said. "Can we use the site?"

It was the first time I'd actually committed myself to the idea. I had no plans. No idea of what exactly I had in mind. It hadn't even been on my mind when I walked into his office. It was as if my mouth were acting on its own. But Misenheimer didn't give his answer any more thought than I had given my question.

"Sure," he said. "Let's see. This is the four hundredth anniversary of the Lost Colony. We'll tie it into that.

"Sure," he repeated. "You can use the site."

I took him at his word. But we weren't tying this into anything. This was no state celebration, no public relations showpiece. This was our homecoming.

The idea of a reunion was nothing new around Creswell and Columbia. Black families had been having them for years. Every summer the Cabarruses had one. So did the Baums. Big get-togethers, with dozens of children, cousins, aunts and uncles streaming in from far-off states and towns as well as from right around home. But they were all separate events, strictly one-family affairs. The Cabarruses would have theirs one weekend, the Baums would have theirs the next. There were plenty of people who attended both—since most of the Baums and Cabarruses are related. But no one ever thought of pulling them all together. No one thought that twenty-one family lines came off that slave plantation, and that that entire group—relatives in blood as well as spirit—deserved a reunion of its own. They

Charlotte Honeyblue Roberts, born in 1853, was twelve years old when she walked from Hurry Scurry to Somerset Place. Her grandson, William Honeyblue, became the mayor of Williamston, North Carolina.

were focused on the living generations, paying little mind to the dead and to the legacy they had left.

Yes, the families have their get-togethers, but the real home-comings around these parts take place at the churches. Salem Missionary Baptist in Columbia. St. John's Missionary Baptist in Creswell. St. Marks A.M.E. Methodist. Disciples of Christ. Come August, they're all booked solid with revivals and reunions, and it's hard to tell one from the other. All the elderly, all the young, all the church members past and present come together for a week of eating, singing and worshiping—not necessarily in that order. Any time of the year, the best bet for reaching black people in a Southern town is through the church. The church is to the black rural South what the town hall was to old New England—a verbal bulletin board, the heart of the community, the place you go to find out who's who and what's what. And for me, August would be the time when it all came together—communities past and present.

I took the entire month of August off from work and moved in with Lee Thomas and Hester Swain, Daddy's cousins, who lived five miles east of Somerset in a place called Chapel Hill. Hard up against the Scuppernong, Chapel Hill was as close as you could get to Columbia and still be "over de river."

That month I spent my weekdays in the Tyrrell and Washington County courthouses and knocking on back country doors, and saving my weekends for church. Before I ever reached a pulpit and began spreading the news of a Somerset reunion, I had to talk to deacons, reverends and pastors, tell them who I was, what I was doing and reserve a spot on a Sunday down the line. Meanwhile, I attended church just like anybody else on any other Sunday—and I got a full taste of what a reunion can be.

The first thing that hits you is, yes, the food. Tables and tables of it, all set up in the wide-open back room you find in every Southern church, the room they call the fellowship hall. Fried chicken, ham, potato salad. Candied yams, stringbeans, butterbeans. Barbecue. Fresh fish fried in a cast-iron pot out back. No pastries or salads or toothpicks. This is down-home country food, the same food you'd see at funerals and weddings.

And there's music. Anybody who's talented in the family performs. Religious music, always religious music. No blues. No rock. But not old-time spirituals either, or gospel in the classic sense. The music would be more an electrified gospel, with amplifiers and electric guitars.

No dancing, no drinking. I've been to plenty of family re-

unions in the city, where everyone checks into a fine hotel, and
you've got partying and drinking, dancing and a bar. But when
you have a homecoming down in these Carolina towns—especially a church homecoming—it's a religious affair. If any drinking's being done, it's being done where nobody sees it.

The first church reunion I went to was at Salem Missionary
Baptist in Columbia. A couple of hundred people were there. I
recognized some of the faces and most of the names. All the
folks who still lived around the area were there, of course, but
others, too. They had the choir from twenty years earlier, back
together and up on the risers, singing. They had a former member who'd come down from New York, where he was teaching
music, and he'd brought along some of his students, all of them
praising God, singing and feasting.

It was the same scene—only with fewer people in smaller
buildings—at the Methodist church and at the Disciples of
Christ. While the Baptists had preserved the whitewashed buildings with tall steeples their ancestors had built, the Methodist
church in Creswell was smaller, more modern, cinderblock and
brick, with leaded windows. And the Disciples of Christ was no
larger than a living room, with a dozen or so rough-hewn, crude,
hand-cut oak pews—pews as old as the church itself, which was
built at the turn of the century. Those pews had to have been
carved by former Somerset slaves.

I'd walk into those smaller churches, listen to the names, look
at the faces and realize I was stepping right back into the Somer-

set slave chapel. The names and the faces were the same—only the generations had changed. There was Odessa Cabarrus and other light-skinned offspring of slave house servants. There was a daughter of Mattie Collins Littlejohn, who married one of the sons of Alpheus Littlejohn, who was Alfred Littlejohn's brother and Fred Littlejohn's son. There was Harold Baum's wife, who was born a Paling—the Palings had been Somerset field hands. There was Jeanette Bennett, who had married a Leigh off the Pettigrew plantation—the same Lees who were ancestors of the young black man, Michael Leigh, who now kept the grounds of the historic site. And there was Jeanette's uncle Ludie Bennett, at eighty-five the oldest member of Creswell's black Methodist congregation.

Ludie Bennett took to me the first day I stepped into that tiny church and started introducing myself around. He's not a big talker. He's never held any kind of formal position. He's worked all his life. But he's as much an elder statesman in Creswell as any aging judge or mayor or senator is in a bigger town. Ludie doesn't have an office, but he's easy to find—every morning he drives through town in a huge green Oldsmobile, parks his battleship of a car at the same corner, climbs onto the beat-up porch of the house on that corner, sits down in one of the tattered chairs on that porch and spends most of the day quietly surveying everything that goes past. And most anything that comes through Creswell does go past Ludie's corner, seeing as how there are only a limited number of corners in a town

Ludie Bennett, son of Darius Bennett, lives with his daughter, Jeanette, in Creswell, but still spends much of his time in the farmhouse where he and his wife lived for fifty years until her death in 1973.

Creswell's size. You want to know something about anything around Creswell, most folks tell you to go ask Ludie.

Like I said, Ludie took to me. And when he heard me asking someone about where I might find a couple of old cemeteries outside town, he pointed the way. It seemed as if he knew where every cemetery—every gravestone—was located for miles around. Ludie had spent his life in these woods and fields, farming, working at a lumber yard and occasionally hiring on at the land around Somerset.

"I farmed over there many, many times," he'd say with a little smile.

He had been living in town with his daughter for years now, but Ludie still spent much of his time in the backwoods farmhouse where he and his wife lived for fifty years, before she died in 1973. A 1973 calendar was still hanging on the wall of the dilapidated old place the first afternoon Ludie took me out there. The roof was caving in—you could see clouds and blue sky through the holes in the ceiling. The place wasn't fit to sleep in, but this is where Ludie would come to be alone, to cook himself a meal and to think. He put a lunch of fried fish, potatoes and corn bread on an old wood-burning stove the first day we went out there.

"Sometimes I just love to get away," he said, setting himself down by the rusty stove. "Sometimes you just want to be by yourself."

Ludie's father Darius had been a Somerset field hand, and Ludie had the look of a hand—dark-skinned, thick-framed, a body made for work. Darius was only a boy when the Civil War began, but his memories stayed vivid until he died in 1948. When Ludie recounted those memories, it was as if they were his own. Through his father's eyes, he saw the well-dressed carriage drivers, the field hands carrying bushels of corn on their heads and the coming of the war.

"When the Civil War broke out," said Ludie, "a lot of 'em was standing in front of the Big House, the lake house. They were told to wait to hear the cannons shoot. When they heard the cannons across the lake, that meant they were in war."

But until the Union troops actually arrived, said Ludie, little changed for the Somerset slaves.

Darius Bennett, born in 1851, was a Somerset field hand. He heard the cannons signaling the beginning of the Civil War.

"I don't know if they knew too much about what was goin' on. All they knew was what the finger pointed at, what they were told to do. You know, just followin' the finger, that's what we call it."

He chuckled, then went on.

"After they broke up the slavery, a lot of 'em got together and come over to Creswell. Freedom of choice, you know. But the Bennetts, when they got free, they all mostly went up and ran away, to New York I think it was."

At one time, said Ludie, there were plenty of Somerset slaves' free-born children in the area. But things had changed over the years, he said.

"The younger ones, they move away. And they's fewer and fewer of us all the time."

Fewer and fewer of us all the time. That was the message I needed to get across to the people in those churches. That we've got to pull together, find the ties that bind and realize that those ties reach backward, far beyond the grandparents who still live and breathe in the back rooms of our homes. My generation is the first one that could think about a gathering of slaves' children. Less than three decades ago this was the officially segregated South. No one would let us lay claim to our ancestors' contribution. And nobody was going to give us credit for it today, just because some laws had changed. That's why it was so important for us to do it ourselves, to be sure that if there is going to be even just one black at a historic event, at a site our people built, that person won't be relegated to the kitchen.

I saw Alex Haley coming to this homecoming. I saw the governor of North Carolina coming. Before I'd ever thought of asking them, I saw them coming. Some things you just know, you just know them intuitively. Some things you do take on a life and meaning of their own, outside of your own life and whatever your own meaning is. I went into those churches, stood up and talked to the people—my people—with a faith they recognized was genuine. Some may not understand my own faith—my beliefs—but they understood the sincerity and belief that came through when I talked about Somerset and our dream.

Religion? Even when I was a little girl, I wasn't always comfortable in the churches I went into, with the faith that put Momma J and my mother on their knees every Sunday. The way they told it, you're in or you're out, you're saved or you're damned. And I just couldn't see life that way. I always felt that we're all connected, that there's nothing I do that doesn't affect someone in South Africa, or someone in China, or you. I couldn't articulate it as a little girl—it was only years later that I learned the universal truths about philosophies that weren't restricted by the name of your church and what type of Christian you were. But even as a little girl, I could see that the churches around me were based on fear, not love. You do good, they taught, or you face the consequences. Even as a child that didn't seem right. I knew there had to be a completely positive approach that could guide my life.

When I got older, I read oriental philosophy. I found the path I could follow. When I was a young woman in New York, I joined a group called the Ethical Culture Society, which met in Lincoln Center. The group was based on a simple principle—that we are obligated to treat everyone as we want to be treated. Blacks and whites alike. When I brought my baby daughter back to Portsmouth, I joined a Unitarian church with the same basic principles. I found a world of philosophies that didn't require chopping people into groups based on their race or religion.

Josiah Collins saw himself as a pious man. So did most antebellum slaveowners. So, I suspect, do most people who act as racists today. Even if they sense a wrongness in their attitude or their actions, they still feel pious because they've got an out, a religious back door that's bothered me ever since I first heard the word: Forgiveness. I grew up being told God will always forgive you. No matter what, God will make it okay. If you do something wrong and ask for forgiveness, you've got it. It wasn't hard for even a little girl to figure out that that kind of lesson gives you the license to do pretty much anything you want.

But what, I asked myself early on, does that do to responsibility? Who ultimately answers for wrong actions? Who pays? I never asked these questions in a vindictive sense. But I wondered what would happen if I knew nobody was going to forgive me if I did somebody or something wrong, that I was going to be responsible, that I was going to feel the negative effects of that action and that those effects were going to ripple out beyond me, causing hurt beyond what I could imagine. If I am going to be responsible for all the pain I cause—to myself and others—if I know that for every action there is a reaction, then my best bet is not to do anything wrong. If negativity breeds negativity and positivity breeds positivity, my choice is easy.

That's why I knew this homecoming was going to happen. The reasons were positive. They were wholesome. They were right. I wasn't going around chanting, "We hate white people because our ancestors were slaves." Those people who owned slaves were dead. I didn't feel a hatred toward them. I felt instead the uplifting surge of a need for our black family to come together. To put all negative baggage behind us and move forward in love. I felt the strength of appreciation, of a love for all the generations who had come before us, who had accomplished so much, who had worked so hard not merely to survive but to enable us to be who we are. There was a pride in all of it. We had come to

202

look at all we have today as if we had just plucked it out of the air, as if we had earned it all ourselves. We had forgotten these people because we were ashamed. But if we'd only remember them, we'd be proud.

These were the things I told the congregations around Creswell and Columbia, week after week, not only during that month I lived there, but afterward, on into 1985, when the idea of a homecoming began to take on the glimmer of reality. At first the older people sitting out in those church pews were skeptical. Interested, but restrained. They couldn't comprehend something like this happening, not at a place where black people had hardly set foot for decades. There had never been a reason for them to go out to that site. To suddenly be told they themselves were the reason was hard to believe.

They had their doubts, until their children and grandchildren arrived on the scene. When the younger generations—the offspring who worked, lived and went to school in other places—came back to church, the older parents and grandparents invariably came through those doors with their chests poked out just a little more than usual. And these kids, the younger generations, they were fascinated by the Somerset story I had to tell—a story they'd never heard—and by the idea of a homecoming. Many of them had been exposed to black history. They had an appreciation for the depth of a past their parents had never heard of. And when the older people saw the kids' enthusiasm, well, that brought more than a few of them around.

By late 1985, the word was spreading—through church, between homes, through letters and over the phone. My own genealogical study was far from finished. I had yet to complete the lists of each family's first generation born free—Poppa Littlejohn's generation. But already the idea of a gathering was taking shape.

We were going to have a homecoming.

SOMERSET
HOMECOMING

No one was getting it.

They were listening, but not hearing, looking, but not seeing. I was sharing nothing less than a vision with the families in and around Creswell and Columbia, some of whom had never been beyond the border of this county, many of whom had never been outside North Carolina. In the steamy churches and on the creaky porches where I spoke, I described a coming together, a gathering that would shatter a century of silence and swell the collective soul of two thousand people. But the faces that looked back at me just nodded and smiled. "That's nice," they said, again and again, with the patience of a mother calming an over-excited child. "That's real nice." Then they'd ask me if I wanted a refill on my lemonade.

They weren't getting it.

Neither were the bureaucratic powers-that-be, the people with the state government in Raleigh. I dropped letter after letter into the black hole of the post office box, with no replies. Not even Bill Edwards at the plantation itself was answering my mail, and the calendar was already turning to 1986—the two hundredth anniversary of the arrival of the eighty Africans at the plantation. This was the year the homecoming had to be held.

No one else shared my vision, but then I was used to that. At work, I'd been bumping into and slipping around bureaucratic walls for years. Some of my staff at the welfare office had master's degrees. They had a hard time taking me or my ideas as seriously as they did their own credentials. When we got a five-hundred-thousand-dollar grant to test ways of sifting through and managing the human problems that staggered into our offices every day—sorting out housing from health care from mental health from crisis intervention and deciding which person needed what first—we applied a medical model from the Vietnam War, triaging our cases the same way the wounded are sorted out on a battlefield: Who stands the best chance of surviving, whose case is the most critical, who can wait, who can't, who won't make it whether we wait or not? My staff didn't think the triage approach would work. But it did—until the grant ran out.

I'd learned long before that the surest way to watch something *not* get done was to drop it in the channel mill, run an idea through planning committees until the life was squeezed out of it, arrange all the right meetings until the meetings become ends in themselves, obey the chain of command so nobody's ego is bruised or—God forbid—somebody's job might look like it's no longer necessary.

Sometimes the approach to a problem is simpler than any system. Sometimes the cue can be taken right off the street: Ain't nothin' to it but to do it. If my people needed a file cabinet, I didn't bother with any work order; I just went on over to Parks and Recreation and said, "You got an extra file cabinet? Well, I need a file cabinet. May I borrow yours?" Same way with desks. And typewriters. And painting: My staff and I were moved into a building that hadn't been touched in years. It was filthy, walls peeling away. Did we requisition to have the offices cleaned and painted, fill out all the proper forms in triplicate and wait? No, we just rolled up our sleeves, went out and bought some brushes and painted those offices ourselves. Not in any institutional off-white beige either. We put in geometric designs. Colors. Five shades of yellow in one room. Palm trees on the wall in another. Shades of pink and flowers. Those rooms stayed dressed in rainbows for three years, until the city finally came through and painted them its way. Three years. That's how long we would have waited in the filth.

We got our best results when there was a spirit of cooperation and support. We were given a one-year grant to set up an employment-based program, to train people on food stamps how to go out and find work. We knew the grant was temporary—but while we had it all we wanted was to get people jobs. People like

207

the Vietnam vet who had worked for Ford, then been laid off, whose hair was all braided and down to his waist, who was so depressed, so lost, so down when he walked through our door that there was no telling what he'd do when he walked out. So the first thing we did was simple. No speeches. No brochures. Just scissors: A beautician in the group cut his hair, right there in the class. No charge. He didn't have money to go to a barbershop. None of the people in that class did. So we cut hair. Then we talked. And we didn't just tell people how to interview for a job, then point them toward the street with a wave and a smile. We drove them to their interviews, walked them to the doors and pumped them up with some words of encouragement. When I wound up before a congressional subcommittee in Washington, D.C., explaining to those politicians how we took this one-year grant and turned out one of the highest job placement rates they'd ever heard of, I told them about those haircuts and pep talks, about how you can't train someone without supporting him too, and how there's no system that can spell out how to give somebody that support. You just do it. You find a way, and you do it.

So I kept writing letters to the state and to the plantation. And I kept driving down to Creswell and Columbia, dropping off stacks of Xeroxed fliers, fifty and a hundred at a time, listing the names I knew were connected to the Somerset slaves and announcing a reunion in August. But it wasn't until a story appeared in the Norfolk newspaper in February that the ground began rumbling.

The story was a big feature—two full pages, lots of photographs. There was nothing in those pages that I hadn't been telling people for three years, no new information, no stunning insights. The article was nothing more than a reflection, a mirror of the things I'd been saying all along. But suddenly my phone was ringing off the hook.

"I read that newspaper story," a voice would say, "and I think I might have kin from down that way."

"Can you send me some information?" another would ask. "I got some people I think need to see this."

The calls and letters came from all up and down the coast, from as far north as Connecticut and as far south as Florida. I'd been talking up the reunion for months, and the word still hadn't reached everybody. But this newspaper article seemed like it was in everyone's hands. Something appears in black and white, on paper, and suddenly it's credible, it's real. People need that, they need tangibility. They need something they can touch, that they can hold, look at, point to. Why that's so important I don't know, but it's honest-to-god necessary for people to feel something with their fingers, not just with their minds. The past is that way—the house you used to live in, the tree you used to climb, the doll you used to take to bed. These are all tactile triggers that fire the emotions in a way mere memories can never do. The day I first stepped onto the ground of Somerset, I felt a tangibility more intense than all the documents and records I'd collected. And I realized now that this would be the power of the homecoming—to bring others to that place and give us *each other* as living monuments, as touchable reminders of the legacy of our shared ancestors.

Tangibility. That's what that newspaper story gave Roy Spruill. Spruill was a retired Baltimore policeman who saw the article, said he grew up outside Creswell, knew some folks up that way who might be connected to the plantation and asked me to send him a couple dozen fliers. One of those fliers ended up in the hands of Clarence W. Blount, Democratic leader of the Maryland state senate. Blount was born down around Creswell, but had moved when he was eight and had not been back. He had no idea he was connected to Somerset. But he was, and now he was eager to come to the reunion, as was Spruill, who chartered a bus to bring himself and thirty descendants down.

Archie Dunbar saw the story. A relative sent a clipping up to Dunbar's home in New London, Connecticut. Dunbar recognized the Baum name in the story, called me and found out his great-great-great-grandfather was James Madison Baum, sold to Collins in 1808. Archie went nuts. He hit every church in the New London area, printed up five thousand fliers of his own, found a couple dozen descendants and lined up a charter bus just like Spruill.

Then there was Gloria. Gloria Lowery Tyrell. Big, dark and solid as a slice of mahogany. She was an actress from Queens— doing everything from one-woman shows on the lives of Harriet Tubman and Martin Luther King, Jr., to clowns. She had an apartment back in Queens filled with a lifelong collection of slave memorabilia, and she had a ten-year-old son with sickle cell anemia. She was on a stage in Norfolk the week the story on Somerset appeared, and she called me the same day. She'd been born in North Carolina, she told me, but she had no connection to Somerset. Still, this was something she had to be a part of. When she headed home that week, it was with a bag full of fliers and my promise that I'd bring her down to help put the event together in August. The busload of descendants that came down from New York was Gloria's doing.

My phone bill jumped to two hundred dollars a month that summer. Suddenly I was no longer the only one reaching out— everyone who called or wrote asked me to find his or her connection to the slaves. My folders of research were falling apart from leafing through them, answering requests to look up ancestors. I realized I had to put the study into a book form— another expense. It would take almost eight thousand dollars to have the study typed and have five hundred copies printed. But I needed those books—when everyone arrived at Somerset, I had to have more than my own tattered notebooks to show them. I told the printer to go ahead. We'd work out the money later.

I began speaking in public. At Norfolk State University, I talked with sociology and history classes about the family and slavery. In Washington, D.C., at Ludie Bennett's daughter's church, I made the same promise I'd begun giving everyone that summer—that North Carolina Governor Jim Martin would be at the homecoming. It was a vow I had no idea might come true. I'd written several times to the state offices, asking about the governor's plans, and had gotten no reply. I'd even written Alex Haley at his home in California, asking him if he could come and if not, if he could at least write the governor in support of the project. Haley did answer my letter—he'd be unavailable for the homecoming, he wrote, since he planned to be at sea on a cargo ship by that time, working on a book. As for a letter to the governor, well, I don't think Haley had time to get around to that.

The state didn't say a thing about the governor, but they finally began sending notes about the event. Once they saw the February newspaper story, which was reprinted in North Carolina papers, Larry Misenheimer and Bill Edwards knew this event was going to happen, and they let me know the state was ready to support it. Soon we were corresponding about details like sizes of trash cans and numbers of folding chairs. Copies of interoffice memos began appearing in my mailbox. Deadly dull paperwork—a sure sign that, in the state government's eyes, this homecoming was happening.

But that was just the beginning. In July I got a call from a Washington *Post* reporter, Barbara Carton. She had seen the February story and saved it. She wondered if the homecoming was still on. We did an interview over the phone, and the end of that month I was sitting at my desk at work when I got a call. It was Barbara, and she sounded ready to pop.

"Dot!" she just about shouted, "We front-paged!"

I went across the street, found a newspaper box and, sure enough, we front-paged. The fact that it was featured in the *Post,* well, I knew what that meant: Even more phone calls and letters would be coming in, now from all across the country. And not just from descendants, but from other papers and magazines as well. I realized now what a chain-reaction one front-page story creates. An editor from *USA Today* called and said, "By God, if the Washington *Post* did a front page, *USA Today* is gonna do a front page." And they did. And by God, if *USA Today* and the Washington *Post* do a front page, then *Time* magazine is going to do a full page. And they did.

It was funny how everything caught fire after that. Reporters came out of the woodwork. Interviews were at least a weekly thing. But they were nothing to be swept up in. All I had my eye on was the homecoming. If it would help the homecoming, I'd do it—television interviews, newspaper interviews, whatever. There was no ego thing to any of this. I've never been one to turn on the TV in the morning and catch the talk shows, and I wouldn't start doing it now, just because I was on them. And I hardly looked at one of those articles that summer. Friends would bring me a copy or send me a clipping of a story about Somerset, but I didn't have the time or the need to look at them. It wasn't for me that those stories were written—it was for the people who had never heard of Somerset, people who might have had connections to the place in body or spirit, and people who simply needed to know that something so positive, so healing, was brewing in a state that was that very summer watching the Klan creep back into its streets.

It was funny to watch reporters from *People* magazine and the

New York *Times* and *National Geographic* slide into the South and suddenly become as down-home as fatback and chitlins. *Time* magazine sent down a senior writer, a real lanky guy with a distinct Southern accent. He said, "Ya know, ah don't usually do this. Ah don't have to go out on the road much anymore." Real laid back. We spent a morning out at the site, then he said, real deep and slow, "Well, the least ah can do is take you out to lunch." By then I was comfortable enough with reporters to just be myself, and the last thing my self wanted right then was to put on a big dog-and-pony show at some fancy lunch spot. I was tired. We passed a Wendy's and I said, "Listen, what do you think of that?" He just beamed: "Ah luuuvvv fast food." So we did burgers for lunch.

The press had a sense of what this homecoming meant, more than many of the people who were closest to it. The reporters recognized the scope, they had the broad perspective. That's their business—perspective. They were looking at it from the outside in, rather than inside out, the way Odessa Cabarrus and the ladies at her church were doing when they got the idea to do some fund-raising at the reunion. They figured they'd cook up some dinner plates to sell the day of the gathering. This was a church with a congregation of no more than fifty. About a dozen of the women, Odessa and her friends, went home, got out their frying pans and cooked up chicken and biscuits—big Southern dinner plates. But they had no sense of the size of the event. They fixed up a few dozen of those plates when it would have

214

taken hundreds to feed the crowd that was coming. They could have cooked for weeks and sold every plate. They just could not comprehend it.

And there were others around town saying, "I'd go, but where you gonna park out there?" Here was a first-in-a-lifetime event, and they were worried about parking.

Some said they had to work that day, and that's what they did. They didn't come, and they only felt the impact of the event later, after it happened, through the eyes of those who made it.

It was a crazy time, the end of that summer. Deborah was out on her own. She had graduated the previous spring, on a day I'd rather forget. My mother and I drove the four hours up to Charlottesville, expecting the dignity and emotion of a traditional black graduation—a choir, solemnity, speeches and tears. What we got was a circus—kids marching down the lawn barefoot under their robes, with balloons tied to their mortarboards, breaking ranks to scream and hug friends, popping champagne corks and leading dogs on leashes. Here was Deborah, my mother's first grandchild to graduate from college, skipping down the grass arm in arm with her sorority sisters as if they were on their way to some picnic. She picked up her degree in international affairs and history, and we all went home, my mother still trying to figure out what she'd just witnessed. Deborah spent that summer with me. That fall she was hired at a community arts center in Portsmouth and moved into an apartment. That winter she was married.

By the next summer, the summer of the homecoming, Deborah had her life and I had mine. In August, I took mine down to Creswell, where I moved into a room in a phoneless hotel, wrote Gloria to come down and join me, and together we readied ourselves for the event, which was now set for—yes, there was irony in the date—Labor Day weekend.

The state had already sent a crew to spruce up Somerset. Carpenters, painters, electricians, groundskeepers—they washed down the old buildings, touched up the mansion's yellow paint and green shutters, and rebuilt steps and porches, shoring up the sturdiness that had withered over the years. Grass was cut, hedges were trimmed, stages were built.

Meanwhile, Gloria and I spent our days at the site and our nights at the hotel, painting signs for the twenty-one family lines, making yellow ribbons to tie around each of the hundred and twenty oaks lining the plantation entrance. I'd already taken care of the other details: preparing the study for the printer, outlining the program for the day's events—from singing of Negro spirituals to enactment of a slave wedding, from Gloria's presentation of her Harriet Tubman show to an African drumming performance, from Senator Blount's speech on the meaning of family to, well, we were counting on the governor giving the keynote address, although we still hadn't heard from his office.

I'd gotten notices from descendants arriving from as far as California and West Germany. The range was staggering. William Brickhouse, thirty-five, an orthopedic surgeon from Richmond would be there. So would William Baum, forty-four, a Rochester chemist. Chef Archie Dunbar, twenty-four, would stand alongside Senator Clarence Blount, sixty-five. And Herman Bonner, forty-five, an aircraft-maintenance engineer, would be there from Portsmouth—not only did Bonner live down the street from me, but we had gone to high school together. Still, we never knew we were cousins until I found our common ancestors on the Somerset slave lists.

The town was changing, too, although I didn't know it. It was Gloria who was always driving into Creswell for a bite to eat at Miss Donnie's, bringing me back something and telling me how one shopkeeper—a white woman—had dug out all her old Nancy Wilson albums and a black doll and had put them all in the window of her store with a sign: "Welcome Somerset Descendants."

All the stores had signs in the windows, said Gloria. And the windows were clean. And best of all, there wasn't a Confederate flag in sight.

Gloria was loving it, riding through town in my big car, driving real slow, smiling and waving at everyone she met, a one-woman parade. "Honey," she'd say, when I'd ask her what she was doing, "they *expect* this from a celebrity."

But most of my time was spent at the site, arranging for all the arrivals and handling the steady stream of interviews. Most of them were the same, but one stood apart—the one that brought me together with Frances Inglis.

In June I'd gotten a call from a producer of the "West 57th" television program. They were planning a piece on the home-coming, to air in February. The woman wanted to come down in August and interview both me and Frances Inglis. I'd heard of Frances, but we'd never met. I knew she was the great-great-granddaughter of Josiah Collins III, the great-granddaughter of George Pompelly Collins, who had run Somerset after his father died during the Civil War. I knew she lived in Edenton, in the house Josiah I had bought on the downtown waterfront. But I had no idea what she was like, how she felt about the plantation and about a black woman stirring up the ghosts of the past. I wondered if I was going to meet a blue-haired daughter of the Confederacy, a stuffy Southern belle who would give the television producers just the kind of confrontation they thrive on.

No way. The woman who approached me that August morning was as fresh and comfortable as the breeze blowing in off Lake Phelps. She was small, in her fifties. Her silver hair was cut short. Instead of makeup she wore a bright smile. Her skirt was cotton and her shoes were simple. There was nothing fancy about her. Nothing pretentious. In her hands she carried a basket made of broom sedge wrapped in split oak that had been made by a Somerset slave. That and a butter knife, she said, were all she had of the Collinses' possessions.

We walked the grounds and chatted. She said she had been as unsure about what I'd be like as I had been about her. She said she wondered if I would come with anger. She said it might seem strange, but she really felt no connection to Somerset Place. Her emotions, her self, she said, were tied to the Edenton house and

218

to her grandfather's house on her mother's side. That house, she said, was no mansion like this. It was a simple country home, with a kiln in the backyard, where she said she still bakes the pottery she makes.

She said she recognized slavery was a fact of life. Her grandmother was a Collins, and her mother had told her the family were good moral people. Frances believed that, she said. But she also felt that however good or bad her ancestors might have been, she is responsible for her own life, not theirs. She was not Josiah Collins, she said. And she didn't live in his time. She could neither condemn, she said, nor defend him.

And I agreed. You inherit your ancestor's genes and their blood, but not their sins or their glories. If they did something wrong, if they lived a life that was stained, you carry forward a sense of guilt only if you're carrying the same attitudes. If the attitudes are gone, there is no need for the shame. That was yesterday, and this is today. Those were those lives, and these are ours.

That, I told Frances, was a focus of the homecoming. That we can live with the past without being dragged down by it. That we cannot deny what happened here—that we must not deny it—and that we must restore this place to reflect all our histories. We were all here before, and so we must all come together again, not just blacks, but whites, too. That's what both Frances and I meant when we talked to each other and to the television reporter about the "healing" of this homecoming.

It was hard for some people to understand what that meant.

219

The week of the homecoming reporters began arriving from all over the country, stalking the Somerset grounds, trying to find someone to talk to. Gloria and I were busy checking lists, painting signs, tying bows and worrying about the weather. It rained on Tuesday, the heat turning the wet air to steam and the ground becoming a mucky quagmire. We were too worried about the mud trapping cars and the heat dropping the elderly to take much time to talk with reporters. But there were enough early arrivals and locals like Ludie to give the writers all the quotes they needed.

One writer, however, looked lost. He was from a Long Island paper, and he was Jewish. He had written a piece earlier in the summer about a group of New York Somerset descendants planning to take a bus to the homecoming. Now he was here to cover the event itself. But he was confused. His family had been victims of the Holocaust. When he had interviewed me for his earlier piece, he had kept mentioning the Holocaust and the horrors of returning to concentration camps. He was filtering this event through his own tragic past. And he was mystified. All around him were people who were laughing, shouting, hugging, celebrating. And he just walked among them, shaking his head and saying, over and over, "I don't understand this. I don't understand why everybody is so up." The day of the homecoming itself, he was just as befuddled. He expected tears of sorrow, of pain. He couldn't grasp that we were finding our roots here, connecting with family, celebrating strength and survival. The

German concentration camps were about horror and death. He saw American slavery only in that light. Slavery *was* horrible, and it was about death. But at Somerset it was also about life. This wasn't a place for killing. We died here, but we also gave birth here. And we grew beyond this place.

I think that's what intrigued the media so much. Many of the more than a hundred newspaper, radio and television reporters who arrived were Southerners. This was a homecoming for them, too. And it was something wholesome, something to be proud of. This wasn't the kind of story they'd come to expect from the South. This wasn't a Klan rally. Or Jesse Helms bristling his political feathers. Or Jerry Falwell preaching fire and brimstone. This was no march, no protest, no fight. This was something warm and real, an event with a genuine gleam, not the PR-posed falseness these reporters had come to expect when they heard the term "event."

Tuesday of that final week I got a phone call at the site. Uncle Fred was dead. He'd lain down the night before, gone to sleep and never woken up. He was eighty-six, and that left Aunt Dot alone, at eighty. Aunt Dot wasn't interested in the homecoming, anymore than she was in all those questions I'd been bothering her with over the past few years. I understood that. But Uncle Fred, he really wanted to come down for the big day. He was hoping to make it, but he'd been feeling pretty bad lately. His system was full of those cleaning chemicals he'd worked with over the years, and they'd taken their toll. Now he was dead. And

I was hurt, but not surprised. It sounds crazy, but my thought when my brother called me with the news was, well, maybe Uncle Fred found a way to be here after all.

Thursday the ground had dried, and it didn't look like rain would be a problem. But the heat—temperatures were in the eighties, there wasn't a cloud in the sky and everything rooted in the ground was wilting. It was funny watching all the reporters walking around in little shorts and sleeveless shirts, trying to adjust to the heat and getting nothing but burned. But I was petrified thinking about Saturday, about the hundreds of family elders who would be coming and how horrible it would be if someone had a heat stroke.

But late Friday the weather broke. I woke up to the coolest morning we'd had since spring. It was so cool the NBC television crew had to scurry around to find warm clothes. They were in a hotel in Williamston, sixty miles away. There aren't too many places to buy clothes in Williamston, and not much choice in the places that do sell them. That day the town was cleaned out of corduroy pants—not designer pants, but country corduroys, baggy awful-looking things.

That morning NBC set up a sunrise interview with me, Frances Inglis and Elsie Baum, who'd lived in Creswell all her seventy-one years and who, like Odessa, believed Charlotte Cabarrus was her great-great grandmother. I'd talked plenty of times with Elsie and told her the truth, and I was going to remind her of it again that morning. But Elsie, well, after all these years she had her story down pat, and it would have been too much to ask her to change it now, in front of the first TV camera she'd seen in her life. So when they asked her about her ancestors, I leaned over and whispered in her ear, "Just tell it the way you always tell it. Tell him about Charlotte."

The rest of that day we got everything in place—put signs out on the roads pointing the way to the site, dodged reporters and —finally—with the help of my oldest brother Fred and my youngest brother Rudolph, tied a yellow ribbon to each of those trees. I went to bed that night with no idea what the next day would bring. So far I'd seen more newspeople than descendants. In the back of my mind I wondered, What if no one came? What if all the people who'd written and called over the last year stayed home? What if they were scared away by all the cameras and reporters? What if the governor didn't make it? What if it rained?

But there was no sense worrying now. I hummed a little bit of an old spiritual to myself: "I Don't Believe You Brought Me This Far to Leave Me." Then I glanced over at Gloria and Deborah and her best friend Kathy, all sound asleep in their beds, and I closed my eyes.

The day dawned like any other at Somerset. A blanket of soft white mist hovered over the fields. The lonely honking of geese echoed from the lake as streaks of pink cracked the gray dawn sky. A moist chill was in the air. That was good. The day would be cool.

Only the state historic sites people were there at 6 A.M., and it was strange walking across the lawn behind the freshly painted mansion, a lawn now covered with rows of chairs, wires, a stage with microphones. Out in the field where the slave quarters once stood, workers had set up a dozen portable toilets. Jesus, I thought, what a place to put those! But everything else looked just right—spare, simple, nothing false or frilly. It was people, not props, that would make this place come alive today.

And it did come alive.

Once the first busload of families pulled up the drive, cheering the yellow ribbons on the trees and stepping out onto the grass—the elderly dressed in their Sunday best, the younger generations in jeans—the day became for me a blur of impressions.

I remember car after car pulling in, everyone grabbing and hugging. People who had never met embracing like lifelong friends. It looked the way a dock does when a steamer comes in, everyone waving and pushing toward one another. Chairs under the arms. Picnic baskets and bags of food in hand.

I remember, as I watched the field fill with cars and buses, someone telling me state troopers were out on the roads between here and Creswell, directing traffic. I hadn't asked for state troopers. But there they were, pitching in, helping out.

And there came the governor, arriving in a helicopter, body guards all around him. Another helicopter flew in, carrying a television news crew. What a sight that must have been for the kids who'd been reared around here, a sight they'd never seen

Dorothy Spruill Redford in the living room of the Somerset Place mansion. A portrait of Josiah Collins III hangs behind her.

before. All these people, and helicopters, and the governor. Somebody said the place hadn't seen so much action since the woods on the other side of the lake caught on fire a few years back.

All the little details I'd worried about had worked themselves out. Dancers, singers, the art show, the actors and actresses, the food and drink were all in place, surrounded by swarms of people, black and white.

Among the whites was Ernestine Liverman, granddaughter of Lloyd Bateman, the overseer who had whipped the Littlejohn runaways during the Civil War. She had driven over from her Elizabeth City home, and she had a copy of my study in her hand. She had read the section about her grandfather, and she said she was hurt. She said she'd always thought of him as a good man. But it was important that she know this, she said, and it was important that she be here, she said, so that no one would hold her responsible for what he had done.

Such a swirl of faces. But I had no idea just how many until I climbed on the stage at ten o'clock to welcome the crowd and introduce the governor. It was then that I looked out on a sea of people, stretching beyond the shade and into the sun, out across the lane that had once kept Josiah Collins' slaves off his yard. More than two thousand people, all come to affirm the bonds most of them never knew they had. There were black children running up and down the steps of the Big House and playing on its porch, the porch their ancestors weren't allowed to touch. There were the elderly, smiling and laughing, but thoughtful, too, ever mindful of the reverence and respect for the past that comes with age.

I saw all this in a blur of motion and emotion. But I couldn't get close enough to any of it to sense the intimacy I hoped everyone else was feeling. For me there was no chance to linger, to savor, to record anything but scattered moments. Ironically, I have the reporters to thank for saving the impressions I was unable to collect for myself. It was not until weeks after that day that I was able to sit down and look through the dozens of newspaper articles written by the reporters who were there. Then, I was able to finally discover just what the day meant to some of the people who had come.

There was Barbara Eason Gadson of Queens, who had grown up forty miles from Somerset, telling a New York reporter, "There were such mixed emotions, living so close all those years and still not knowing we had any ties to the place. Now, I don't feel bitterness. I feel we are found!"

There was Urmilla Davidson Smith, also of Queens, who had grown up in Tarboro, eighty miles from Somerset, telling the same reporter, "How can I put it? The immigrants all went through Ellis Island, but we weren't immigrants. Now we know where *we* started."

There was my brother Fred, telling a reporter how he spent his early boyhood in Columbia and how he remembered a group of drunken whites forcing him to jump into a canal, one of the canals dug by the Somerset slaves. "I was more afraid of them than the water," he said, "so I jumped." I'd never heard that story before, but then there's so much I've still never heard, so much for everyone to tell.

There was Josiah Collins VI, great-grandson of Josiah III, who had flown in from Seattle after Frances had called him. A retired real estate broker and appraiser, the seventy-eight-year-old Collins seemed overwhelmed by the gathering. "I had no idea it would be like this," he told a reporter from a Los Angeles paper. He told the reporter how his father had moved west, settling in Seattle to practice law, and how he himself felt little connection to Somerset.

"My father was born at Somerset Place in 1864," said Collins.

"His only recollection of the place was a story about taking quinine because of the malaria threat from mosquitoes. He was about five years old when he lived there, and he told a story about hiding outside under a hydrangea bush every morning until his nanny came to get him and made him go in the house for his coffee. They put quinine in his coffee. My father never drank coffee again after he left the place."

I wondered who his nanny was.

There was Cecil Rouson, Jr., father of New York Giants running back Cecil "Lee" Rouson III, talking about running into James Blount, whom he grew up with in Elizabeth City. "I've known him all my life," said Cecil, "and I just found out today we're second cousins."

And there was Cecil's cousin Bill, who flew in from Riverside, California, with his fifteen-year-old son Itiri Songo. Bill was standing with his two brothers and sisters and several cousins he had found as he described his feelings. "This is kind of eerie, everyone being related," he said. "But it has to do with people not being so remorseful about slavery, but reaching for a heritage. Not dwelling on the hurtful things, but looking for something positive. I just feel good about it. I think this has made a lot of people feel good about themselves."

There was Sam Poole from Maryland describing "a feeling of warmth, of connection and an indescribable feeling of joy."

And there was Roy Spruill telling a Philadelphia reporter a story I couldn't believe had now found its way into print. "My grandmother used to talk about the old days," said Roy, remembering the slave quarters that had been torn down by the time he was a boy. "The slave shacks are all gone now, but they were wooden and built with wooden pegs. The rumor was that when it rained you could see the blood reappear from the beatings in the old days."

There was Harriet Spruill Hill, walking across the grounds with a large group of family, telling a reporter, "You know, this is my first time up here, and I grew up six miles away."

There was Edward Felton, a supervisor at the District of Columbia Rehabilitation Services Administration, telling a Washington *Post* reporter, "If these trees could talk, I'm sure they'd tell stories that would bring tears to my eyes."

And his wife, Zora, director of education for the Smithsonian's Anacostia Museum in Southeast Washington, saying, "I have been so moved. It's like I have talked with Harriet Tubman as I walked these grounds."

There was Senator Blount, talking about his mixed feelings of sadness and celebration. "I suppose there is still some embarrassment," he said of any reminders of slavery. "I'm sure our country is embarrassed. But we don't feel embarrassment here. Think about the strength it took to build this place. Talk about true grit; talk about the right stuff. They had it—and so do we."

There were voices of disappointment, like that of Ethel Dickson, who drove down from Washington, D.C. "Frankly," she said, "I feel that something is missing. It's kind of hard to have strong feelings about this place, because everything is gone that reminds you of slavery."

But her husband, Edward, a microbiologist at Walter Reed Army Medical Center, disagreed. "I feel warm and emotional," he said. "I had planned to check out my roots and when I found out that someone already had done it, I was very excited."

There was Dr. Valerie Hornablue, who had come from Williamsburg, Virginia, with her husband, Dr. Richard Hornablue. "For so long, slaves have been portrayed as stupid and lazy," she said. "But it took some smart and hard-working people to put this together." She mentioned that she and her husband had recently bought an old plantation back in Virginia, "And not once," she laughed, "did we consider asking whites to work on it."

230

There was another doctor, William Brickhouse of Richmond, standing next to a neighbor he had discovered was his kin through the Somerset lines. "It is very exciting to get this close to history," said Brickhouse. "Reading about slavery doesn't evoke any real emotion. Being here helps internalize it, gives us something to hold on to."

There was Willis Phelps of Norfolk saying, "Today I can tell my children where I came from. No more will I have to say I came from Africa. I am from Washington County—Creswell. I have roots."

And there was his daughter, Carolyn Phelps Benton, saying, "My children have begun asking questions. They know nothing about slavery. I will have a lot of explaining to do when I get home."

There was North Carolina governor Jim Martin asking the crowd, "Did you hear it? Did you hear the sound in your head calling you home?"

And, yes, there was Ludie Bennett, putting it all in perspective for a Virginia newspaper. "We don't look back in hatred," said Ludie. "We look forward in freedom."

By the middle of the afternoon, the day had a momentum of its own. Clusters of people—white and black—moved among one another, strolling on the grass, walking down to the lake, passing in and out of the mansion's rooms. As I stood watching the performance of the slave wedding ceremony, I felt a tap on my shoulder. I turned around, and there was Alex Haley, standing with a couple of friends and smiling at me. I screamed and grabbed that poor man, squeezing the life out of him. It turned out he'd gotten off his ship in Antwerp, Belgium, and was on a plane headed to Los Angeles when he'd seen a newspaper story about the reunion. On impulse, he said, he picked up a couple of friends, flew to Norfolk, rented a car, and here he was.

It was so appropriate that Haley had come, that he was a part of it now, since he had, in a sense, been a part of it from the beginning. The funny thing is no one had even noticed Haley before I threw my arms around him. After that, everyone recognized him. He was mobbed the rest of the day, as I guess he is wherever he goes. Before he left, we found a few minutes alone in one of the mansion's rooms, and Haley warned me about letting all this attention get in the way of the goals I'd had when I

231

began. "After today," he told me, "your life will no longer be your own."

The only sadness in the day was Gloria's. All morning she was searching for the bus from New York that was supposed to arrive with fifty descendants and her son. By mid-afternoon, some of the older guests were already folding up their chairs and heading back to their cars and buses. The day was winding down, and still the New Yorkers hadn't arrived. By four o'clock, most of the crowd had said their good-byes and were gone. Then, finally, the bus arrived, limping up the drive. Gloria's son was carried off. The heat and the long trip had pushed him into sickle-cell crisis. Gloria hustled him into a car and left for the hospital in Elizabeth City, where he was cooled off and cared for. The rest of the group was unfurling celebration messages they had spray-painted on bedsheets, getting all the hugs they could and happily accepting what was left of the food. Their bus, they said, had broken down somewhere around Baltimore. It had taken them all day to make it, but they weren't about to give up. And they did make it, if only for an hour.

By six the only people left on the site were reporters and state workers, who had given their all that day. The grounds were spotless. Not even a cigarette butt was left on the grass. But then what else would anyone expect? This was sacred ground now, the home of our ancestors.

The day was over. The sky was already darkening over the eastern horizon. I walked out across the field where the slave

232

cabins had once stood. And I turned and looked toward the mansion and outbuildings, now smeared with late afternoon shadows. So many shadows.

I thought back to how this all began, to the loneliness I'd felt when I'd first sat down with Mother, to her parents, who had made a life for themselves in a tiny town I'd never known, to the discovery of a world that history books had never shown me—a world of colonial businessmen whose success depended on shrewdness and whose shrewdness included their ability to treat humans as commodities. I thought back to the day I first found this place in the woods, and to the story that unfolded once I was here, to the ghosts I discovered, the family I found and the relatives I now knew I had.

And I thought of my own family, the people through whom I had begun this journey. I thought of Aunt Dot, poor Aunt Dot. Alone now, without her husband and without the past she had chosen to erase from her life. I thought of Uncle Fred, who would have been so overwhelmingly proud of this day—not surprised, but proud.

And I thought of my mother, who, through the grace of some miracle, was able to find a flight from New York and Uncle Fred's funeral on Friday to Somerset on Saturday. For her, this day was a blessing, a comfort after her brother's death, which had hit her hard, harder than anyone else's could have. She had a husband and children, but Uncle Fred was her brother, her only link to her own past. When he died, she was devastated. Had the home-

233

coming not occurred when it did, the grieving process would have lasted much longer. But this gave her something to replace the grief.

And there was something more. Something subtle. There was a change in how Mother saw me. You see, as much as Mother was excited about my work, about the family we were all discovering, there was still a gap between us—a gap that had to do with God. When it came to judging a person's worth, Mother always went by the book—the Good Book. She always judged a person based on church attendance, and I'd fallen short of the mark for years. She'd always thought I was good, but she never thought I was righteous.

After the homecoming, however, she started looking at me a little differently. She was absolutely convinced all this could not have happened without God's blessing. The way it came together, the perfectness of the day and of all that had led to it— Mother figured there *must* have been some divine intervention there. She figured God must have been looking on me with a favorable eye. And so, for the first time in my life, in terms of the spirit, Mother was looking on me with that same favorable eye.

And Daddy? He took in the day like all his boys did. He and my brothers, they were jubilant, full of pride, stroking me and stroking themselves. The Spruill men, they saw that day together—the first time they'd gotten together like that as adults. They were a group, roaming the grounds shoulder to shoulder, to the extent that the women who came with two of my brothers were really upset. They felt ignored. The guys weren't paying attention to them. But then, this was more than a date.

And there was something that happened with my sister Lethia. Some months later, we found a moment alone together, and she started talking about the day I'd come back to Virginia, back when I was eleven. We'd never talked about it before. I knew what I'd seen and felt, but I never knew how *she* saw it. Again, I'd never asked.

She told me how really anxious and excited she'd been about my coming, how she wanted so much to have someone to play with, to share her bedroom with. And then, when she saw me, with my Peter Pan hat, my little blue suit, my patent leather shoes, my head stuck up in the air—she was crushed. I was not what she'd hoped for. The friend she had hoped for never arrived. And the hurt had stayed for years.

But now we were healing the hurt, talking like we'd never talked before. Lethia had an art degree from Pratt Institute. She had a world to offer me, and that day she began bringing me into that world—and I began bringing her into mine.

So much had blossomed that day. As I watched the sun set over those cypresses, I thought of what people really mean when they talk about destiny. This was my destiny. I began as a woman alone, drifting in both time and space. But now I had a past peopled with links as strong and as solid as any family in this nation. I was anchored. And I had a present cluttered with relatives, with blood kin. Now there is no place I can go that I can't find somebody I'm connected to, someone I belong to.

The need to belong. That's what this was all about. Not just my need, but the need of our entire people, whose destiny was out of our hands for so long, and who are still struggling to shape our identity, our sense of place in a society that was not of our making. In the beginning, when we were first brought to these shores against our wills, our strength was in our selves, in our bonds with one another. Somewhere along the line, in complex and subtle ways, those selves were severed, the bonds broken. My journey, climaxed on this day, was a reunion in every sense of the word.

And, I realized as the sky turned purple and the hum of evening insects rose from the swamp, the journey is not yet over, for me or for any other black man, woman or child who has not found the family that will save him or her from drifting into the oblivion of a rootless world. This was a day, one day. But there was more to do here at Somerset. Here, I knew, was an opportunity for more than a picnic. Here was a place, a chance to build a monument to the lives and labor of my family, a monument that would remind others of what their families did at other places just like it all across the South. I could see a completely reconstructed, working plantation rising from this ground. The barn rebuilt as it once was, with oxen once again pulling carts. Water, clear and strong, flowing once again through the canal. The gardens lush and full. The church standing once more, its pews as they were when my ancestors sat in them. The tools wielded by the black artisans in place again. And the homes of the slaves themselves, standing and glowing with the aura of life that once filled their rooms.

I walked back toward the buildings, where the state people were packing up their cars for the drive back to Raleigh. Larry Misenheimer was there, and I took him aside.

"Larry," I said. "Look around you. Larry, I don't know if you remember, but when I first mentioned this homecoming, you didn't really respond. You didn't take it seriously."

I paused, and I turned toward the empty field by the lake.

"Larry," I said. "We're going to build those slave quarters."

I paused again.

"And Larry," I said. "Please take me seriously this time."

237

A
H O M E C O M I N G
P O R T F O L I O

State of North Carolina

JAMES G. MARTIN
GOVERNOR

SOMERSET HOMECOMING DAY

1986

BY THE GOVERNOR OF THE STATE OF NORTH CAROLINA

A PROCLAMATION

Two hundred years ago this summer, eighty Africans arrived at Edenton aboard the brig "Camden," bound for slavery at Somerset plantation in Washington County, North Carolina. There they joined other slaves in carving out a prosperous plantation from a swampland, enduring the inhumane hardships of grueling, hazardous work as well as a life of bondage in a foreign land with an unfamiliar language.

These slaves and their descendants are recognized as having made significant contributions to North Carolina and the United States. They persevered in the new land under harsh conditions, developing an unique culture that remains a part of the American fabric. With the long-awaited abolition of slavery, the Somerset plantation slaves dispersed throughout this nation, in many cases losing ties with family members and the state.

Now, more than 120 years after receiving their freedom, and through the genealogical research of Mrs. Dorothy Spruill Redford, thousands of Somerset slave descendants will rekindle family bonds at a Homecoming at the Somerset Place State Historic Site on August 30th.

NOW, THEREFORE, I, JAMES G. MARTIN, Governor of the State of North Carolina, do hereby proclaim August 30, 1986, as "Somerset Homecoming Day," a day to mark the many contributions of the slaves and their descendants, and foster a healing of historic abuses by promoting life and family.

IN WITNESS WHEREOF, I have hereunto set my hand and affixed the Great Seal of the State of North Carolina at the Capitol in Raleigh this twenty-eighth day of July in the year of our Lord nineteen hundred and eighty-six, and of the Independence of the United States of America the two hundred and tenth.

JAMES G. MARTIN

Dorothy and author Alex Haley at the homecoming. It was the television production of Alex Haley's Roots *that inspired Dorothy to find her own.*

Dorothy and Governor James G. Martin of North Carolina.

Dorothy and her daughter Deborah at the site of the slave quarters at Somerset Place on the morning of the homecoming.

247

Actress Gloria Lowery Tyrell as Harriet Tubman.

248

Kathy Young jumps backward over a broom in a reenactment of a slave wedding.

250

From left to right: Barbara Eason Gadson, Geraldine Beal Preston, Urmila Davidson-Smith, and Minne Preston Bramwell. For Barbara Eason Gadson, the reunion was a bittersweet dream, a moment to walk across the fields of the plantation where, four generations ago, her ancestors worked in bondage. "We are found!" exclaimed Gadson.

251

Newsday/Daniel Sheehan

252

Musician Jeffrey Littlejohn plays his guitar amid the cypresses at Somerset Place.

Josiah Collins VI attended the homecoming reunion.

256

257

Gertrude Norman, of Pea Ridge,
North Carolina, watches the home-
coming celebration from the porch
of the Somerset Place mansion.

EPILOGUE

I t's been a year now since the reunion, and I have a new home
—in Creswell.

Funny the twists and turns a life can take. Funny how things
can come full circle. So many in my family spent more than a
century drifting away from this place, shutting out the past,
forgetting. And now here I am, moving my life back here, open-
ing doors, remembering.

I live right on main street, across from Ludie's corner. I can
wake up, look out my bedroom window and there he is, settled
into his favorite chair, watching the world go by.

My bedroom is one of eight in this house—two stories, eight
rooms, all for a hundred and fifty dollars a month.

The house, like almost everyone and everything else in Creswell, is linked to Somerset and to my own family. It was built
around the turn of the century by Lonnie Spruill, son of a Petti-

grew slave named Jordan Spruill. Among Lonnie's children was Roy Spruill—the same Roy Spruill whose fliers about the homecoming ended up in Senator Blount's hands. Harriett Spruill Hill, who lived but six miles from the plantation and had never been there until the homecoming, was Lonnie's daughter.

The last woman to live in this house was a woman named Lilly Spruill. Momma J's brother, Setan, was once madly in love with Lilly. In fact, Setan was returning from a visit to Lilly's the day Pappy Jenkins, Momma Letha and a Columbia woman named Rayponsa met him at the door to the Jenkins house. Rayponsa was pregnant by Setan, and that's why there was one other person there to greet Setan when he got home—the preacher.

Some of Lilly's things were still in the house when I got here—family photos and such—so I felt at home. Lilly hadn't lived here for some time, and the house showed it. The front porch leaned a bit, paint was peeling, the staircase had no banister. It never did. Sunlight shone through some of the slits in the wooden walls, and a crawling vine grew through a living room floorboard, sending shoots of green up the wall behind the sofa. But once the dust and dirt were swept away and my things moved in, I had a house with heart—the heart that comes from the past. There were realtors who, when they heard I was moving down, tried showing me larger, finer homes on acreage outside town. But I wasn't interested in living out on some estate. I came down here for my people, and I meant to live among them.

You see, I still have work to do.

Larry Misenheimer did take me seriously this time. The state decided to develop the Somerset site, to re-create the conditions and community of the slaves who lived there, and I was hired to take charge of the project. Now it's both Bill Edwards and I who are steering Somerset. And there is so much to do. I want these grounds to be a model, an inspiration to other blacks whose families came off other plantations to realize their history and search for their own slave ancestors. And I want this to be a source of records and research for the hundreds of Somerset descendants who have yet to discover their past. This will be more than an inert monument; it will be a living museum.

The cabins will come first, built slowly, one by one, of the same size and shape and on the same spots where they originally stood. People will walk into them as they can now walk into the Collins mansion. And they will know who lived here, which room Old Suck actually sat in when she gathered her clan around her, which house Fred Littlejohn slept in with his wife and children. They will know the work these slaves did and how they did it—the sweat and the skill of these men and women.

And there is still so much work to be done with my research. I still get a couple of letters and phone calls each week from someone looking for links to Somerset or asking me how to begin his or her own genealogical journey.

The publicity from the homecoming continued to ripple for weeks after the event. I appeared on several television programs, including "Good Morning America," where guest host

Ronald Reagan, Jr., interviewed me, poking for anger that wasn't there. I taped a program for a North Carolina PBS station and appeared on Charles Kuralt's Sunday morning show. Stories on the event ran in newspapers from here to Hawaii and overseas. Just the other week a friend handed me a Somerset story that appeared in a Finnish newspaper. I've got no one to translate it, but I've got a good idea what it says. Another friend said he'd heard a radio report on the homecoming while traveling in Africa. So word did get around.

It will never stop spreading if I can help it. There will be another homecoming in August 1988, this time bringing in the descendants of the eighty-one Collins slaves who were shipped to Alabama in 1843. I've already located hundreds of Alabama addresses in places like Selma, Birmingham, Uniontown, Demopolis, Orrville and a village called Browns, where a group of thirty Bennetts live not ten miles from the plantation their Somerset ancestors arrived at almost a hundred and fifty years ago.

The cycle of letters, fliers and phone calls has started again— to the Alabama descendants and to the dozens of other Somerset offspring who have surfaced across the country since last year.

I'm home now. Home like I've never been home before. I'll be out front working on the house, and kids will walk over from yards down the road. Shy. Curious. They ask me if I'm going to be living in this house, where did I come from, do I have any kids. Most of all, they want to know, do I have any kids.

"Yes," I tell them. "And I've got a grandchild."

Julyan Murphy, Deborah's five-month-old son. Before he was born, my daughter looked at all this as her mother's strange obsession. But now she's got that little boy gazing up at her with those shiny wet eyes. And suddenly, she's stitching our family tree, the limbs climbing back seven generations, to hang on her little boy's wall. The feelings she has, the feelings I have, are the same feelings Senator Blount described in a letter he sent me after the homecoming:

> I have lived long, been many places, have seen and done much—but never in my wildest dreams would I have thought that this experience of "discovery" and the unleashing of my roots could nor would so profoundly and positively affect me. I feel good! I feel proud! I feel redeemed! I understand me and mine a little better. For the first time in my life, I love me in a way I've never loved me before. For the first time in my life, I love my parents and grandparents and those before them in a way I never knew them, nor loved them before. I feel close to the families involved though I never knew of them.
>
> I have always been proud of who I am. And I have always appreciated the little part of me that I know. But now I have a new found appreciation of "from whence I have come." And a new vision where I, and we as a people, must go. And now I know *why* we must go.

Amen, brother.

SOURCES

"Books Belonging to Josiah Collins, Nathaniel Allen and Samuel Dickinson, Equal Co-Partners in Sundry Tracts of Land Taken Up and Purchased in Tyrrell County, 1785–1790." In *Annie S. Graham Papers,* North Carolina State Archives.

Fouts, Raymond Parker. *Abstracts from Newspapers of Edenton, Fayetteville and Hillsborough, North Carolina, 1795–1800.* Edenton Chamber of Commerce, 1984.

———. *Abstracts from the State Gazette of North Carolina.* Vols. I–III. Edenton Chamber of Commerce, 1982.

Genovese, Eugene D. *Roll, Jordan, Roll; The World the Slaves Made.* Vintage Books, 1976.

Gutman, Herbert G. *The Black Family in Slavery and Freedom, 1750–1965.* Vintage Books, 1977.

Johnson, Guion-Griffin. *Ante-Bellum North Carolina.* University of North Carolina Press, 1937.

The Josiah Collins Papers. Private collection. North Carolina State Archives.

Kay, Marvin L. Michael, and Cary, Lorin Lee. "Slave Runaways in Colonial North America, 1748–1775." In *North Carolina Historical Review,* January 1986, pp. 1–39.

Lemmon, Sarah McCullough, ed. *The Pettigrew Papers,* Vol. I, 1685–1818. North Carolina State Archives, Department of Archives and History, 1971.

Littlejohn family history. In *North Carolina Historical and Genealogical Register.* Vol. I, No. 2. April 1900, pp. 268–83.

Mannix, Daniel Pratt. *Black Cargos: A History of the Atlantic Slave Trade.* Viking Press, 1962.

Parramore, Dr. Thomas C. *Cradle of the Colony: The History of Chowan County and Edenton, North Carolina.* Edenton Chamber of Commerce, 1967.

Poole, William C. "An Economic Interpretation of the Ratification of the Federal Constitution in North Carolina." In *North Carolina Historical Review,* No. 22, 1950.

Powell, William S. *Dictionary of North Carolina Biography.* Vol. I. University of North Carolina Press, 1979, pp. 404–6.

Ruffin, Edmund. "Jottings Down in the Swamp." In *Farmer's Register,* No. 12, 1839, pp. 702–3, 724–32.

Styron, William. *The Confessions of Nat Turner.* Random House, 1967.

Tarlton, William S. *Somerset Place and Its Restoration.* 1954. Unpublished study prepared for the Division of State Parks, North Carolina, Dept. of Conservation and Development.

Transcript of Uriah Bennett testimony. In *Farm Security Papers.* North Carolina State Archives, 1937.

WPA slave narratives. In *The Slave Community, Plantation Life in the Antebellum South,* by John Blassingame. Oxford University Press, 1979.

Wall, Bennett Harrison. *Ebenezer Pettigrew, An Economic Study of an Antebellum Planter.* 1946. Unpublished dissertation at the University of North Carolina, Chapel Hill.

Wood, Peter. "Digging Up Slave History." In *Southern Exposure,* March–April 1983, pp. 62–65.

Bills of sale and deeds of trust found in the Chowan County Office of Register of Deeds.

Birth, marriage and death records registered in the Washington County Office of Register of Deeds.

Dates of slave births, baptisms, marriages and deaths recorded in the parish register of St. David's Chapel. North Carolina State Archives.

PHOTO CREDITS